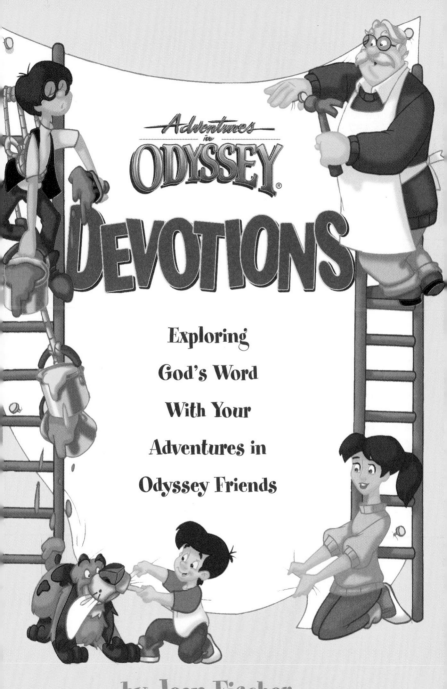

Adventures in ODYSSEY

DEVOTIONS

**Exploring
God's Word
With Your
Adventures in
Odyssey Friends**

by Jean Fischer

with Heather Hardison

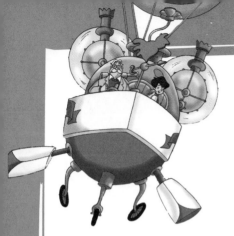

Published in Nashville, Tennessee, Tommy Nelson®, a division of
Thomas Nelson, Inc.

Adventures in Odyssey and the Adventures in Odyssey logo are registered
trademarks of Focus on the Family, Colorado Springs, CO 80995

ISBN 1-56179-888-6

Printed in the United States of America
00 01 02 03 04 05 RRD 9 8 7 6 5 4 3 2 1

Where Do I Start?

Welcome to Odyssey, a small American town where people will smile at you and say "hello" even if you're a stranger to them. We're not too fancy or formal at my soda shop, but we all have one common goal: to help you learn to live your faith. That's why we designed the *Adventures in Odyssey® Devotions* book just for you!

Here you will find learning units gathered into simple three-page sections, each focusing on its own theme. Now, some of you might like to read just the devotion and its Bible passage, then wait till the next day to move forward. Others may want to read a whole unit at once.

What's important is that you enjoy learning at your own pace. Join Dylan, Connie, Jesse, Eugene, and me in the places we love best, doing what we love best: learning to grow with God. We think you'll find that each day you spend with your devotions will lead you to more and more adventures in Odyssey.

Mr. Whittaker

Table of Contents

Dylan

Holly

Sherman

Whit

Eugene

Sal & Carter

God Knows Us

It was a warm night in Odyssey. Mr. Whittaker and Jesse were outside looking at the sky. "Mr. Whittaker," Jesse said, "how many stars are there?"

Psalm 8:3-

"I'm not sure anyone knows," Mr. Whittaker answered.

Jesse was quiet for a while. "There's just so much of everything!" she said. "How can God know all of us?"

"That's easy," Whit said. "God knows us because He made us and He loves us. And you never forget someone you love."

Does the great, big world ever make you feel small? It helps to remember that God made you and He loves you.

WORD FOR THE DAY

CREATION

The Bible begins with the Creation—the six days in which God created the whole universe.

It tells us that God made everything in the sky and on the earth. He made every kind of plant and animal. And, best of all, God made people, just like you and me.

Memorize Me

So God created man in His own image; in the image of God He created him; male and female He created them.

GENESIS 1:27

A Little Prayer

Dear God,

Thank you, Lord, for all of the wonderful things that you've made. Help me to remember when the world seems so big that you know me and you love me.

Amen.

WHIT'S CORNER

Creation

GENESIS 1

Have you ever noticed that the best place to start something is the beginning? If we want to make a tree house, we need wood, nails, and a hammer. But the first thing we need is a tree. A tree is the beginning of a tree house.

God thought the best place to start was the beginning, too. But God is so powerful, He started with nothing. There wasn't anything until He made it. And then, He created everything just the way He wanted it.

God created us, too. He made the first family and told them to have lots of children. That's where we came from. We're God's children. God also told the first family to take care of the earth.

We can do this in many ways. When we work in a garden and grow food, we're taking care of the earth. We also care for it when we help rake leaves and when we feed and love our pets. How else can we take care of God's earth?

Waking Up Thankful

"It's a beautiful summer day," Holly's mother said. "It's time to get up now."

Ecclesiastes 11:7

Holly rolled over in bed. "I'm still sleepy," she groaned.

"You must've stayed up late reading again," her mom said as she opened the curtains to let in the sunshine.

Holly could hear the birds singing. And she could smell lilacs in the breeze from her bedroom window. Her mother was right. It was a beautiful day.

As she got out of bed, Holly whispered this little prayer:

"I'm thankful for this day, Lord, even though I'm sleepy!"

Do you have days when you don't want to get out of bed? Try to remember that every day is a gift from God.

WORD FOR THE DAY

REJOICE

Did you know that rejoice means "to be happy"? God wants us to be happy about the wonderful things He does. So open your eyes and ears, and see and hear what God has done. Take time to look and listen. And remember to rejoice! How? There are lots of different ways. You can say a prayer. You can sing a song to the Lord. You can even draw a picture of something you saw or heard. However you rejoice, you'll show God that you are happy with Him and that you are thankful for the things He has done.

A Little Prayer

Dear Lord,
Thank you for creating this day. The things I see and hear make me happy. Thank you for the sunshine, the birds, and the flowers. Thank you, too, for my family and my friends. When I feel too sleepy to get up in the morning, Lord,
please help me to remember that every day is a special gift from you.
Amen.

Memorize Me

This is the day which the Lord has made; We will rejoice and be glad in it.

PSALM 118:24

Being Kind

"Hurry up, Dylan," his mother said. "Mr. Nelson is waiting."

Matthew 10:40–4?

"Do I have to go to the nursing home with you?" Dylan whined. "Everyone there is old."

"They haven't always been old," Mrs. Taylor said. "If you spent time talking to Mr. Nelson, you'd know that he used to play professional baseball."

"Really?" said Dylan.

When he thought about it, Dylan knew that he hadn't been paying attention. If he had tried to get to know Mr. Nelson, they would already be good friends. Maybe they still could be!

God made each of us in His image—not just our friends and family members. It's important to remember this when we meet new people, no matter how different they seem.

A Little Prayer

Dear Lord,
Help me to be kind to everyone I meet. And please help me to remember that everyone needs love and understanding.
Amen.

WORD FOR THE DAY

KIND

Are you *kind*? If you are, then you are loving and helpful toward others. That means your little brother, the bully down the street, and also the lady next door. God says that it doesn't matter who the other person is. He wants us to be kind to *everyone*.

DID YOU KNOW?

HELPING OTHERS

Did you know that the Bible teaches us about being kind? In Matthew 10:40–42, it says that whenever we help someone, something good happens. It doesn't matter how small or unimportant the person seems. God created each person in His own image, and He sees each act of kindness.

Remember—each time you help another person, God says that you've helped Him. So, if you want to do something to help the Lord today, be kind to someone!

Memorize Me

"And whoever gives one of these little ones only a cup of cold water in the name of a disciple, assuredly, I say to you, he shall by no means lose his reward."
MATTHEW 10:42

Thanks, God!

Daniel 6:10

Dylan gave Sherman a scoop of ice cream.

"That may not be the wisest thing to do," said Eugene. "You're teaching him bad habits."

"It's just ice cream," Dylan answered.

"Nevertheless, ice cream has little nutritional value for an animal. It would be a much better habit if . . . "

"There's no such thing as a *better* habit," Dylan interrupted.

"Yes, there is," said Eugene. "For dogs, chewing a rawhide bone might be a good habit. And for us,

praying every day is definitely a good habit."

"I never thought about that," Dylan answered. "I always thought that habits were bad."

Praying is a great way to say thanks to God, and it's a wonderful habit to get into.

A Little Prayer

Dear God,

I thank you for the wonderful things you do for me. Please forgive me for my bad habits. I know that praying is a good habit, and I will try to remember to say my prayers every day. And I will always try to remember to say thank you.

Amen

Memorize Me

In everything give thanks; for this is the will of God in Christ Jesus for you.

1 THESSALONIANS 5:18

WORD FOR THE DAY

THANKFUL

When we're *thankful*, we're pleased. We aren't just thankful for things we get. We're usually thankful to the person who gave them to us. When you think about it, every good thing comes from God. So, we have a lot to thank Him for. One way to thank God is to say a prayer. Eugene told Dylan that prayer is a good habit. And prayer is a *great* way to show that you're thankful.

Setting Priorities

Eugene didn't notice when Connie and Mr. Whittaker came into the lab one night.

"There you are!" said Connie. "We've been looking for you."

"Where else would I be?" Eugene replied. "I've been working on this ionization chamber."

Luke 11:4

"We missed you at Bible study," Connie answered softly.

Eugene's face went blank. "Uh-oh! I meant to come," he said. "But I got caught up working on my ionization chamber, and I just forgot!"

"It's important to set priorities and stick to them," Whit said. "We need to be careful that nothing gets in the way of our relationship with God."

Nothing is more important than God. We should always try to put Him first. Always.

A Little Prayer

Dear God,
Sometimes I forget to put you first. Please help me to stay away from temptation. I want you to be more important than anything else in my life.
Amen.

WORD FOR THE DAY

POSSESSIONS

Your possessions are everything that you own. That means your toys, your clothing, your allowance, your pets—everything! God wants us to put Him before everything we have.

WHIT'S CORNER

Putting God First

LUKE 18:18–2?

I want to tell you a story from the Bible. One day a very wealthy man asked Jesus how to get to heaven. Jesus told him to obey God's commandments. The man said that he had. So Jesus told him to sell everything he owned and give his money to the poor.

Well, this man didn't want to give away all his money. So Jesus told him it would be easier for a camel to fit through the eye of a needle, than for a rich man to get into heaven. Jesus was trying to show the man that it's impossible to get into heaven if you don't put God first in your life.

Some people make money the most important thing in their lives. Others may put their jobs or favorite hobbies first. Many things feel important, but God is the most important. When we put Him first, we become more like Him. And we take a step toward heaven.

Do the Right Thing

Dylan flew by Connie so fast that he almost knocked her over.

"What's going on?" Connie asked.

Proverbs 3:7

"Some of the kids broke a window," Dylan answered, "and we all ran away."

"Why did you run away?" Connie wondered aloud.

"It happened so fast," Dylan said. "When everybody started running, I did too."

"Do you think that was the right thing to do?" Connie said.

"No," Dylan answered, looking down at his sneakers, "but if I go back, I might get in trouble!"

"Yes, you might, Dylan," Connie answered.

It's easy to follow our friends. But God wants us to stop and think hard before we do something wrong. Even when it's tough, God always wants us to take responsibility for our actions.

✦ A Little Prayer ✦

Dear Jesus,
Sometimes I don't think about what you want me to do. Instead, I follow my friends. Help me to always do what is right—even if it's not what my friends would do.
Amen.

WORD FOR THE DAY

FOLLOW
When you follow someone, it means that you do what they do or say to do—like follow the leader. Jesus is the best leader of all. If you remember to follow Him, you will stay out of trouble.

DID YOU KNOW?

DON'T ALWAYS FOLLOW THE LEADER

Did you know that you shouldn't follow the leader if the leader does something wrong?

In Proverbs 3:7, King Solomon gives good advice. He says that we shouldn't do what we want to do. Instead we should think about what God would do. If we behave as God would, we will stay out of trouble.

Dylan didn't stop to think before he ran away. Instead, he did what his friends did. It's okay to be part of a group. It's fun to do things with your friends. But Proverbs warns us not to follow our friends into doing something wrong.

God's Great Love

"What are you doing out here, Eugene?" Whit wondered. "It's a cold night for star gazing."

"I'm studying Jupiter, Mr. Whittaker. This is a perfect time to observe it."

1 John 3:1

Whit looked through Eugene's telescope. "It's amazing how close it looks," he said.

"What amazes me," added Eugene, "is how big the sky is. Imagine all that's out there that we'll never understand."

"And God's love for us is even bigger than the sky," Whit answered. "We know that for sure."

"And we don't need a telescope to see it," Eugene said.

Whenever things seem too big to understand, we can always know God's love.

A Little Prayer

Dear God,
I know that your love for me is so great. I believe that Jesus is my Savior, and I'm happy to be one of your children.
Amen.

WORD FOR THE DAY

GREAT

When something is *great,* it's wonderful and magnificent. That's how we can describe God's love for us. It is the most wonderful and magnificent thing that there is. God's love is so great that we cannot even imagine it. Aren't you glad that He loves you so much?

DID YOU KNOW?

GOD'S CHILDREN

Do you know anyone who was adopted? Adopted children weren't born into their families. Instead, their parents chose them. Then they became their adoptive parents' own children, just as though they were born into their families.

Jesus came here so that we could all become one family together. Do you believe that Jesus is your Savior? If you do, then you are one of God's own children, reborn into His family.

You already know how much God loves His children. His love is bigger than the sky. It's wonderful to know someone loves you that much!

Memorize Me

Behold what manner of love the Father has bestowed on us, that we should be called children of God!
1 John 3:1

God Cares

"Hey, Sal," Dylan said to his friend. "Do you wanna try this new ice-cream flavor that we invented?"

"No," said Sal. "I don't feel like it."

1 John 4:16

"What?" Whit laughed. "You never refuse to test our new flavors."

"I've had a bad day," said Sal. "I lost my lunchbox, I did bad on my spelling test, and it rained on me when I walked over here. And *nobody* cares!"

"Sure they do, Sal," Whit said. "Dylan and I care. But what's more important—God cares. Nobody loves you more than He does."

Always remember God's love for you. He cares about your problems—even those that nobody else even knows about!

A Little Prayer

Dear God,

I know that you care about what happens to me. On the days when I feel like nobody cares about me, help me to remember how much you care. Your love is greater than anything. It is even bigger than the sky. Thank you, God, for loving me.

Amen.

Memorize Me

And now abide faith, hope, love, these three; but the greatest of these is love.

1 CORINTHIANS 13:13

WORD FOR THE DAY

LOVE

When you love someone, you care about him or her very much. But there's more to love than that. First Corinthians, chapter 13 says that love is kind and that it isn't jealous. It says love is never rude. Love isn't selfish, either. And love doesn't think evil thoughts. Love never fails; it's always there and full of hope.

Best of all, Corinthians says that there is nothing greater than love. God's love is the greatest thing there is!

Even when you feel like nobody cares, the way Sal did, you can be sure that God cares. And even if you think **you** don't care, God cares! Isn't that cool?

God Is Always There

"Dylan says that you're going to Bible camp with him," Whit said to Carter.

Romans 8:35–39

Carter grinned. "Yeah. We're leaving this afternoon."

"You'll have fun," Whit answered. "How long will you be gone?"

"A whole week! And I'm kinda scared. I've never been away from home that long."

"Don't worry," said Whit. "Your parents are only a phone call away. And you know who else is with you."

"Who?" Carter wondered.

"God!" Mr. Whittaker said. "He's there whenever you need Him."

Do you feel worried and scared sometimes? Remember that you're never alone. God is always with you.

A Little Prayer

Dear God,
I'm so glad that I can count on your love.
When I'm alone, I won't be afraid, because I know that you're right here with me.
Amen.

WORD FOR THE DAY

ALWAYS

Always means forever. Do you know how long forever is? Nobody does, because forever has no beginning and no ending. Forever is like every day and every night, but longer. God will always love you, and He will always be with you. You can count on Him to be there for you day and night—always!

DID YOU KNOW?

GOD IS RIGHT HERE

Have you ever been separated from your mother or father? If you have, you probably felt afraid, just like Carter did.

But did you know that God is always with you? You don't have to worry about being separated from Him.

Romans 8 tells us that *nothing* can separate us from God's love. No matter where you go, God is right there.

He knows where you are every minute of the day, and He knows just what's happening to you. God's love will be with you—no matter

> ## Memorize Me
>
> "Lo, I am with you always, even to the end of the age."
> MATTHEW 28:20

what—and it will help you feel safe and cozy. You can depend on it.

That Makes Me Mad!

The door crashed open. Dylan came into Whit's End, trying hard to hold onto Sherman.

"What's wrong?" Whit asked.

"That Jesse makes me so mad!" Dylan answered. "She let Sherman run through the mud. He's a mess."

"Do you know what happened yesterday?" Whit asked. "I had just mopped the floor, and somebody with dirty shoes came in. There were muddy footprints everywhere."

"Whoops," Dylan blushed. "That was me. Are you mad at me?"

"Of course not," Whit answered. "Now are you still mad at Jesse?"

Whit forgave Dylan even though Dylan didn't ask him to. But when we make a mistake or sin, we ask for God's forgiveness. He doesn't stay mad at us, either. He forgives us right away!

⋆ A Little Prayer ⋆

Dear God,
Forgive me when I do bad things. I will try harder to do what's right. Help me, also, to forgive the people who do bad things to me. Amen.

WORD FOR THE DAY

MERCY

Mercy is forgiving kindness. God has mercy on us. When we ask His forgiveness, He gives it in a kind and loving way. Do you have mercy on people who are unkind to you? That's exactly what God wants you to do! You should forgive them with mercy right away.

DID YOU KNOW?

GOD IS FORGIVING

Did you know that God gave Adam and Eve a beautiful garden to live in? There was only one rule—not to eat the fruit from one of the trees. Adam and Eve ate the fruit anyway. And their sin made God very angry.

We are all like Adam and Eve. We all do sinful things. But there is good news! God says that if we believe His Son Jesus Christ is our Savior, He will have mercy on us when we do something wrong. God wants us to forgive each other the same way that Whit forgave Dylan.

Memorize Me

For as the heavens are high above the earth, So great is His mercy toward those who fear Him.
PSALM 103:11

God Is Very Wise

Connie had a project for all the girls to do at Bible camp. "Everyone bring your white shirt and come with me," Connie

Galatians 5:22–23

said, showing them tubs filled with different colored dyes.

"Pick a color," she said. "If you want your shirt to be pale, leave it in only a few minutes. But if you want it bright, leave it in a lot longer. The more time the shirt is in the dye, the brighter it will be."

The more time we spend with God, the brighter we can shine for Him.

FUN TO DO:

Get an old box and decorate it like a treasure chest. Next, ask your parents to help you cut different colors of paper to look like big jewels. On each "jewel," write a different way God helps us to be wise. You might begin with, "Treat other people the way I want them to treat me." What are some other ways to be wise?

A Little Prayer

Dear God,
I know your wisdom is like a treasure, and the more time I spend with you, the wiser I will be. Thanks for making me shine!
Amen.

WORD FOR THE DAY

KNOWLEDGE

Proverbs 2:6 says that knowledge comes from God. When you have knowledge, it means that you know about something. God wants you to know more about Him. The best way to do that is to spend time with God. When you pray and read your Bible, God will give you more knowledge about who He is.

WHIT'S  CORNER

Wisdom

You know, the Bible is full of stories about so many different people. Do you remember the story of the three wise men who came to see baby Jesus in Bethlehem? They followed a bright star and brought special gifts.

PROVERBS 2

The Bible calls these men wise. But you don't have to know a lot about stars to be wise though. You don't have to be all grown up and bring presents, either. But you do have to know God. Knowing God takes patience and time, like when the girls wanted their shirts to be brighter.

Remember, He's the only one who can give us wisdom. And the Bible says we should search for it like it's a hidden treasure. Wouldn't it be neat to find a hidden treasure? Well, finding wisdom is even better. Only, it's not so hard to find. It's in your Bible. And if you ask God for help, it will also be in your heart.

Faith Is Like Gold

DEVOTION

"See my ring?" said Connie.

"How pretty," Whit answered.

Proverbs 3:5–6

"It's gold," Connie told him.

"Gold is expensive," Eugene added. "It becomes pure when it's exposed to high temperatures. There's nothing like pure gold."

"Oh, but there is," Whit answered. "Our faith is like gold. The bad times we have are like a fire. They make our faith strong and pure."

"I never thought about it that way," said Connie. "Bad times can be good for us. They make us depend on God."

God will help you in bad times. Trust His love, and pray to Him. He will help your faith to become pure and strong, like gold.

A Little Prayer

Dear God,

Even when things go wrong, I will trust in you. I know, God, that you love me and that you will protect me. In bad times, instead of thinking that you are far away from me, I will remember that you are always close by. Amen

Memorize Me

Trust in the LORD with all your heart, and lean not on your own understanding; in all your ways acknowledge Him, and He will direct your paths.

PROVERBS 3:5

WORD FOR THE DAY

FAITH

Faith means "trusting and believing in someone or something." You have *faith* that your parents will love and take care of you. But faith in God isn't always this easy. When times are tough, it can be hard work to use our faith. God does love us. And He will take care of us. We show our faith when we remember this.

Last spring, when Jesse and I were playing in the attic, a thunderstorm started. Then the power went out. Jesse got so scared. I reminded her that God would take care of us. And we said a little prayer. Then we carefully went back downstairs. When the power went out again this fall, Jesse wasn't even afraid! She knew she was safe.

Just like Whit says, having faith through our problems is like a purifying fire. God rewards our trust in Him by making our faith stronger!

Thanks For Everything

"You look sad, Dylan," said Whit.

"I didn't get the part in the play. Seth got it." Dylan answered.

"Did he deserve it?" Whit asked.

1 Thessalonians 5:16–18

"Yeah, I guess he did," Dylan replied.

"God always has a good reason for the things that He does," Whit said. "I think you should thank Him for choosing Seth."

"Thank Him?" Dylan cried.

"That's right," Whit answered. "The Bible says that we should thank God for *all* things—the good things and the bad. We *always* play a part in His perfect plan."

God doesn't make mistakes. He always does what's best for us, even when we don't understand what He's doing.

A Little Prayer

Dear God,

Thank you for everything. Even when it feels like you answer "no" to my prayers, I know you have reasons that I don't have to understand. I will keep on praying, and I will try to be happy with everything that you do for me. Thanks for knowing what's best!

Amen.

WORD FOR THE DAY

CEASING

The Bible says that we should pray without *ceasing*. This means "without stopping." Especially when we are thankful, we remember to pray with joy. But, when things go wrong, we should not stop praying then, either. Instead, we should pray even harder and ask God to help us.

DID YOU KNOW?

WHEN THINGS GO WRONG

Did you know that when we believe in God during hard times, we show Him that we have faith in Him? If you want to learn more about it, read Hebrews 11. This entire chapter is about people who had great faith in God, even when things went wrong. Without a doubt, these people were winners. They trusted God and they were thankful—even for things that they didn't understand.

Sometimes it's hard to be thankful when things don't go your way. But God can use your faith to make this easier for you.

> ## Memorize Me
> Rejoice always, pray without ceasing, in everything give thanks; for this is the will of God in Christ Jesus for you.
> 1 THESSALONIANS 5:16–18

Merci Beaucoup!

"Merci beaucoup," Eugene said.

"Merci beaucoup?" she asked.

"Yes, Miss Kendall. It's French *for* thank you."

Matthew 6:7–8

"I know what it means, Eugene," Connie said. "But why not just say 'thank you'?"

"Because everyone says 'thank you,'" Eugene answered. "I wanted you to know I really meant it."

"Well, it worked. And you know what, Eugene?"

"What, Connie?"

"You're welcome," she answered. "And I meant that, too!"

God doesn't want us to say the same old thing every

time we pray. He wants us to say what we really mean each time. So, try to think of some new ways to thank God.

WORD FOR THE DAY

HEATHEN

In Jesus' time, people who did not believe in the God of the Bible were called heathens.

A Little Prayer

Dear God,
I am going to sing you a special song today.
And I know that you're listening:
    Father, lead me day by day,
    Ever in Your own sweet way;
    Teach me to be pure and true;
    Show me what I ought to do.
Amen.

WHIT'S  CORNER

Singing to God

Last summer, when we had a big thunder-storm in Odyssey, the power went out for a long time. Dylan and some other kids were here, and we played about fifteen games of checkers.

Finally, Dylan asked, "What are we going to do now, Mr. Whittaker?" I thought for a moment, and I took down a hymnal from the bookshelves. We sang our favorite songs for the rest of the day.

God loves to hear us sing. It doesn't matter if you sing with others or by yourself. Good or bad—loud or soft— He'll hear you. But don't wait to get started. Sing a song of thanks and praise right now!

FUN To Do:

Try singing your bedtime prayers. Just think of your favorite song, and sing your prayer to its tune.

What's on the Inside?

Connie noticed that Holly looked angry. "Is everything okay?" Connie asked.

1 Samuel 16:7

"The kids at school have been teasing me," Holly said. "They call me carrot top."

Connie smiled. "You have beautiful hair," she said. "People used to say that to me, too. I think it's because not many people have red hair. So just remember how special you are."

"I guess you're right," Holly said happily.

It's easy to spend time worrying about how we look. But God wants us to think about who we are on the inside. Being kind, honest, and good—these are the things that really matter in our lives.

A Little Prayer

Dear Lord,

Help me not to worry about what I look like. Help me to grow strong in my heart. When other people tease me about the way I look or the way I act, help me to remember that it's what's in my heart that counts.

Amen.

Memorize Me

For the LORD does not see as man sees, for man looks at the outward appearance, but the LORD looks at the heart.

1 SAMUEL 16:7

WORD FOR THE DAY

CHARACTER

A person's *character* is made up of things like honesty, loyalty, kindness, and a willingness to try. Character is what's inside us. When the kids at school teased Holly, they were only seeing what she looks like on the outside. Another part of character is courage. We sure can feel that on the inside! Now, Holly doesn't even worry when someone teases her. She has always had courage—but she's learned how to use it to protect her feelings. If somebody calls her "carrot top," she has the courage to just ignore that person. She knows she has great hair to match her great character!

Our bodies will some day grow old and wear out, but our character—the person we are on the inside—can continue to grow better and stronger for all of our lives.

Be a Good Example

"What happened to you?" Connie asked. Dylan's shirt was covered with yellow smudges.

"Mark Stout," Dylan answered sadly.

1 Timothy 4:12

"Dylan," Connie giggled. "You smell like a ham sandwich!"

"I do not!" said Dylan. "Mark wanted me to steal a kid's lunch money. When I said that I wouldn't, he rubbed mustard on my shirt."

"You do sort of smell like a deli," Whit chuckled warmly, "but I'm glad to have a friend who stands up for what is right. You were a good example for others, just like God wants us to be."

God wants you to be a good example. He'll help you to make the right choices.

WORD FOR THE DAY

EXAMPLE

An *example* is something that we can choose to be or follow. Doing something good sets a good example. Doing something bad sets a bad example.

A Little Prayer

Dear God,

Help me to always do what's right. I want to make good choices and to be a good example for others.

Amen.

Memorize Me

Let no one despise your youth, but be an example to the believers in word, in conduct, in love, in spirit, in faith, in purity.

1 TIMOTHY 4:12

WHIT'S  CORNER

Growing in Faith

1 TIMOTHY 4:12

Way back when I was a kid, sometimes I felt too small to make a difference. Other times I felt like nobody even noticed me. I want you to know that God notices everything about you. He thinks you're very important. In His kingdom, it doesn't matter how young you are.

That's what the Bible says in 1 Timothy 4:12. It says that young people are important. When people forget to treat you like you're important, God wants you to be an example for them. When you're honest and polite and try to help others, people will notice. And it will remind them how to do what's right and good.

The Bible says we can be an example with our words. That means saying nice things to other people, even when we're angry with them. It also says to be an example in the way we live. That can mean lots of things!

God Knows Everything

On Sunday morning, Dylan remembered that his spelling test was the next day.

Proverbs 11:17–20

Oh no, he thought, *I want to play with my friends after church. Mom and Dad will make me stay home if I haven't studied yet!*

Then he had an idea. He put his spelling words in his Bible.

"I'll just study them during Sunday School," he said aloud, pleased with his plan. "No one will ever notice."

But in Sunday school, Dylan was studying spelling when it was his turn to read. He didn't know where to start, and he was

embarrassed. Everyone noticed when it happened—and God noticed, too.

God always knows what's in our hearts. He sees our sin, and He wants us to be honest.

A Little Prayer

Dear God,

I know that you see everything I do. Sometimes I sin, even when I try not to. Please forgive me, Lord, because I am honestly sorry. I know that you love me, and I will try my best to be a good example for others. Amen.

Memorize Me

All we like sheep have gone astray; We have turned, every one, to his own way; And the LORD has laid on Him the iniquity of us all.

ISAIAH 53:6

WORD FOR THE DAY

SIN

Sin is when we think that what we want is more important than what God wants. We sin whenever we do something wrong. All of us sin, no matter how good we try to be.

Sometimes we make mistakes and have accidents. These usually aren't sins. If you get confused about your actions—whether you are sinning or just making a mistake—don't ever be afraid to ask your parent or Sunday School teacher about it. God wants us to understand what sin is. And He doesn't mind when we have accidents.

The Bible compares sinners to sheep that have run away. But it also says that Jesus is like a shepherd. He wants to find us and help us to be good examples again. So, whenever you sin, tell God that you apologize. Be honest with Him all the time, because God knows everything that's in your heart. He will always forgive you.

It's Okay to Cry

DEVOTION

Jesse sat on the chair reading a sad story. It was about a little girl who didn't have any friends. A tear ran down Jesse's cheek, and she made a sniffling sound.

John 11:35

"Jesse!" her mother called from the kitchen. Jesse could hear her mother's footsteps coming. Just before her mom got to the living room, Jesse hid her face behind her book.

"Are you having trouble reading?" asked her mother.

"No," Jesse answered. "I don't want anyone to see me crying."

"Jesse, don't be embarrassed," said Mrs. Taylor. "You're reading a sad story. Your tears just help show that you have a kind heart."

The Bible tells us that even Jesus cried, so don't be afraid to show your feelings. He understands, and He'll always listen.

✦ A Little Prayer ✦

Dear God,

I feel better knowing that you understand how I feel. Thank you for always being there when I am sad or disappointed. When my feelings are hurt, it makes me feel better just knowing that you love me. And help me not to be embarrassed to cry, because even Jesus cried sometimes.

Amen.

WORD FOR THE DAY

WEEP

To *weep* means to cry. The Bible says that Jesus wept, which means that He was weeping, or crying. The Bible also says that there is a time to cry, just like there is a time to laugh.

DID YOU KNOW?

SHOW YOUR FEELINGS

Did you know that "Jesus wept" is the shortest verse in the Bible? But those two words can teach us a lot. They show us that an important part of Jesus' character was His willingness to show His feelings. There are many stories in the Bible that describe Jesus showing other feelings, too—sadness, forgiveness, love, disappointment, and even anger.

So, don't hide your feelings from God. Be honest with Him. Jesus had many of the same problems that you have, and God will understand. Like Mr. Whittaker says, God is always waiting to hear from us and to help us.

Do You Care?

DEVOTION

The kitchen at the Taylor's house was a mess. Mr. Taylor and Jesse were working hard on some sort of project.

1 John 2:10

"What are you making?" Mrs. Taylor asked as she came in the back door.

"It's a cake for Dylan's birthday," Jesse told her. "It was my idea."

"Well, I'm certain that Dylan will appreciate your kindness," her mom said.

"And God will, too," said her dad. "He likes it when people do nice things for each other."

God loves it when we show people that we care about them. "I love you" is a good thing to say to your family members. Try it today, and see what happens.

WORD FOR THE DAY

ABIDE

Abide means to stay. The Bible says that we should abide in the light. The light is the light of God. If we abide in His light, it means that we are staying with God and trusting in Him.

A Little Prayer

Dear God,

Thank you for caring about me! I do love my family and friends. Help me to find ways to show them that I care. And when others are nice to me, I want to let them know I'm glad. Amen.

Memorize Me

If we love one another, God abides in us, and His love has been perfected in us.
1 JOHN 4:12

DID YOU KNOW?

THE STORY OF JOSEPH

Did you know that it's important to show your family that you care?

Have you read the story of Joseph? His brothers were very mean to him, and they sold him to be a slave. Eventually, Joseph became one of the main rulers in all of Egypt. Even though his brothers had been terrible to him, Joseph forgave them. He even kept loving them.

A long time later, Joseph saw his brother Benjamin for the first time in many years. Benjamin knew immediately that Joseph still loved him, because Joseph was so glad to see his brother that he cried.

Jesse said "I love you" to Dylan by making him a cake. Can you invent other ways to say "I love you" to your family and friends?

Honor Your Father and Mother

Deuteronomy 5:16

Jesse wanted to go out to play, but her mom asked her to stay in. They almost had an argument, but then Jesse remembered something.

"I'm sorry, Mom," she said. "In Sunday School we learned to honor our father and mother. So I'll stay inside, just like you want me to."

Jesse did the right thing! Later, they made brownies—much better than being upset!

Do you always do what your parents tell you to do? The Bible says that it is important to honor your father and your mother. It's so important that God made it one of His commandments.

WORD FOR THE DAY

HONOR

When you *honor* your parents, it means that you show them respect with your behavior and words.
Behaving with honor is being kind, helping out, trying not to argue, and all kinds of other good behaviors!

A Little Prayer

Dear God,

I know that my parents love me. Please help me always to honor and obey them.

Forgive me when I misbehave, and help me remember to apologize when I should.

Amen.

Memorize Me

Honor your father and your mother, as the LORD your God has commanded you.
DEUTERONOMY 5:16

WHIT'S CORNER

Parents Need God

2 KINGS 5

I bet your parents have taught you lots of things. They probably helped you learn your ABC's and how to count to ten. Maybe they taught you how to remember the names of all the books in the Bible. Or perhaps they helped you learn how to make chocolate chip cookies.

There's a Bible story about a child who helped grown-ups. It's the story of a man named Naaman, who got very sick. His wife had a little servant girl who knew that only God could make Naaman better. One day, the girl told him that he should go see God's prophet, Elisha.

And when Naaman did what Elisha asked him to do, he became well again. Only the little girl knew that God was the answer to Naaman's problem. God is the answer to our problems too. He's always here for you— and your parents. He knows no one is too young to help others learn about Him.

Getting Even

Dylan stormed into Whit's End. "That's it!" he said, "It's time to get even."

"Get even with whom?" Whit asked.

Ephesians 4:31–32

"Rodney let the air out of my tires."

"Are you sure it was him?" Whit asked.

"It's something he would do," said Dylan. "He does mean stuff a lot."

"Well, making plans to get even with him isn't the right thing to do," Whit said. "God wants us to love our enemies, even if we don't know who they are. Now let's go pump up those tires."

God wants us to be kind and forgiving to people, even those we don't like or know.

WORD FOR THE DAY

VENGEANCE

Vengeance is a big word that means "getting even." In Leviticus 19:18, God says that we should not take vengeance on anyone. That means that we shouldn't try to get even when someone does something bad to us.

A Little Prayer

Dear Lord,
It's hard sometimes to love the people who are mean to me. Please help me to forgive these people and to treat them as I want to be treated. Amen.

Memorize Me

And be kind to one another, tenderhearted, forgiving one another, just as God in Christ forgave you.
EPHESIANS 4:32

DiD YoU KNoW?

LOVING OUR ENEMIES

Did you know that in Leviticus 19:18, God tells us, "You shall not take vengeance, nor bear any grudge against the children of your people, but you shall love your neighbor as yourself; I am the LORD."

When others criticize you or make you feel bad, it's natural to want to get even—just like Dylan wanted to get even with Rodney. Try to notice feelings like this, and think about them. This can be tough, but you can do it. God says that we must love other people *even* when they are mean to us.

So, the next time someone is unkind to you, remember God's words. Don't try to get even. Instead treat them with kindness. You can do it!

The Hardest Kind of Prayer

Holly came into the ice-cream parlor and threw her backpack on the table.

"Bad day?" Connie asked.

"Amy Reed makes me so mad," Holly answered. "She tripped me when I got off the bus."

Luke 6:27–28

"That wasn't very nice of her," Connie said. "What are you going to do about it?"

"I haven't decided," Holly answered.

"I think you should pray for her," Connie suggested.

"Pray for her!" Holly cried.

"*Sometimes* it's a hard thing to do," Connie said. "But it's what Jesus told us to do. Give it a try."

God wants us to pray for our enemies. He knows that it isn't easy, but that's what He wants us to do. God will help you to find the right words. And He will bless you for obeying Him!

A Little Prayer

Dear Lord,
I know that you don't want me to hate my enemies. So, please, Lord, bless the people who might hurt me. Forgive them for being unkind to me, and help me to treat them in a kind and loving way. Amen.

Memorize Me

"But I say to you, love your enemies, bless those who curse you, do good to those who hate you, and pray for those who spitefully use you and persecute you."
MATTHEW 5:44

Bless those who persecute you; bless and do not curse.
ROMANS 12:14

WORD FOR THE DAY

PRAYER

Prayer is talking with God. There are different kinds of prayers. We can pray to thank God. We can ask for things that we want and need. We can pray for other people, too. Praying for other people is important, because God wants us to love and care for everyone.

The hardest kind of prayers are those for people we don't like. Jesus said, "Pray for your enemies." That can be tough! But we have to remember to do it.

Holly and I prayed together for Amy. And we both felt better when we did. Why don't you give it a try? Pray for someone who hasn't been nice to you. See if it doesn't make you feel better.

Making Things Right

Jesse must have asked Dylan a hundred times to play checkers on her new checkerboard. But Dylan didn't want to play. Finally, Jesse grabbed him by the arm, and she pulled hard. "Play with me!" she wailed.

Matthew 5:9

Dylan got mad. He threw the checkerboard, and it broke.

Then Jesse started to cry. She cried hard.

Dylan felt just awful. "I'm really sorry, Jesse," Dylan said. "I didn't mean to make you cry."

We all do things that hurt other people's feelings. When that happens, it's important to say that we're sorry. Apologizing won't fix what we've already done, but it can help to make everyone feel a lot better.

A Little Prayer

Dear God,
Please forgive me for hurting other people's feelings. I don't mean to do it, but sometimes it just happens. Please help me remember to apologize, too. Thanks, God. Amen.

WORD FOR THE DAY

PEACEMAKERS

Peacemakers are people who try to make things right. When they do something wrong, they apologize for it. When they see a fight or argument starting, they try to make peace instead. God wants all of us to act like peacemakers.

DID YOU KNOW?

THE STORY OF ABIGAIL

Did you know that an apology can stop a fight? In the Bible, Abigail's husband, Nabal, was rude to King David. That made the king angry, so he decided to start a fight. An apology would have stopped things, but Nabal wouldn't say, "I'm sorry."

Abigail knew that a fight would be terrible. So, she brought dinner to the king's men. It was dangerous for her to do. The men were so angry that they might have killed her! Still, Abigail took the chance. She apologized for her husband's behavior.

King David accepted the apology, and he promised not to fight. Can you imagine what might have happened if there was no apology?

Memorize Me

"Blessed are the peacemakers, For they shall be called sons of God."
MATTHEW 5:9

A Second Chance

DEVOTION

"I never thought it would happen in a million years," Carter said.

"Yeah, I wonder what he's up to," Dylan answered.

"Who are you talking about?" Whit asked.

Matthew 18:21–22

"Jerry," Carter said. "Dylan left his lunchbox on the bus, and Jerry returned it."

"Yeah," Dylan chimed in. "And Jerry *never* does anything nice. So we think he's up to something."

"Maybe you should give him a second chance," Whit suggested. "He might be trying to change."

When people do bad things over and over, it's hard to trust them. And it's even harder to forgive them.

But people can change! God wants us to be forgiving and give people a second chance.

A Little Prayer

Dear Lord,
Help me to forgive people who might hurt me,
and help me to give them a second chance.
Amen.

WORD FOR THE DAY

PERSECUTE

Persecute means to hurt people. Early Christians were often persecuted by people who didn't understand that Jesus had come to save the world.

Memorize Me

Lord, how often shall my brother sin against me, and I forgive him? Up to seven times? Jesus said to him, "I do not say to you, up to seven times, but up to seventy times seven."

MATTHEW 18:21-22

DID YOU KNOW?

THE STORY OF SAUL

Did you know that Saul was a man who hated Christians? He didn't believe in Jesus. Then, one day, a miracle happened.

Saul was on his way to capture Christians and punish them for worshipping Jesus. While he was walking, he heard Jesus' voice. It said, "Saul, Saul, why are you persecuting Me?" Saul knew that it was Jesus speaking, and he was very frightened. Right then and there, Saul knew that Jesus was real. Saul became a believer!

Soon he became the apostle Paul, and he worked for the Lord as a disciple for the rest of his life.

So, you see, people can change.

A Beautiful Attitude

Jesse and Dylan had a huge fight over the TV.

"I always watch *this* show," said Jesse, pushing the channel button back to her program.

Matthew 5

"I don't care," Dylan answered, clicking the remote back to his channel. "My favorite show is on *now*."

Mrs. Taylor turned off the television. Dylan and Jesse were both very quiet. "Your attitudes are terrible today," Mom said softly. "Think about how God wants you to behave."

Jesus taught the Beatitudes, so we would know how to behave. If we learn and follow these lessons, we will bless others with beautiful attitudes!

A Little Prayer

Dear God,

Thank you for your blessings. And thank you for your Son and His Beatitudes. Please help me to remember how you want me to behave. And please give me strength to always do what's right.

Amen.

WORD FOR THE DAY

ATTITUDE

Your *attitude* is the way that you feel about something. If you have a good attitude, you will probably be in a good mood.

Memorize Me

"Blessed are the pure in heart,
For they shall see God."
MATTHEW 5:8

WHIT'S CORNER

The Beatitudes

In the Beatitudes, Jesus tells us that He blesses people for certain behaviors and situations. For the most part, the Beatitudes are about being nice, kind, humble, and good.

MATTHEW 5

They also say to love everyone, even people who are mean. God wants us to be nice to mean people. He doesn't want us to get angry with them. We can help them by praying that they let God into their hearts.

There are still other important Beatitudes: Remember to trust God. He doesn't want you to worry. And don't forget to ask for His help when you need it. God knows we make mistakes, and He's always there to take care of us.

FUN TO DO:

Read the Beatitudes in Matthew 5 with your parents. Ask them to explain things you don't understand. Then talk with them about different ways to have a beautiful attitude each day.

Putting Others First

DEVOTION

"What's wrong, Dylan?" Whit asked.

"Kyle asked me to help with his science project," Dylan said. "If he doesn't get a good grade, his mom won't let him play baseball."

Matthew 16:24–25

"So what's the problem?" Whit asked.

"If Kyle doesn't play, then I get to be shortstop. I've always that position."

"What are you going to do?" asked Whit.

"I'll help him out," Dylan answered.

Whit agreed.

Dylan sighed. "It's not always easy to put others first. I sure want to be shortstop."

God wants us to put others' needs before those of our own.

A Little Prayer

Dear God,

I want to remember to put you first, other people second, and myself last. That's hard to do sometimes, but I'll try.

Amen.

WORD FOR THE DAY

JOY

Joy is the way you feel when you're very happy. When we remember to put God first, then others, then ourselves, we find that our joy gets bigger. It is a lot like love; the more joy given, the more received!

Memorize Me

" . . . do not worry, saying, 'What shall we eat?' or 'What shall we drink?' or 'What shall we wear?'

" . . . Your heavenly Father knows that you need all these things. But seek first the kingdom of God and His righteousness, and all these things shall be added to you.

MATTHEW 6:31-33

DID YOU KNOW?

Did you know that I've invented a way to remember to put Jesus and other people first? Would you like to know how? Just remember how to spell JOY. The first letter, "J", stands for *Jesus*. The second letter, "O", stands for *others*. And the third letter, "Y", stands for *yourself*. When you put Jesus first, others second, and yourself last, then you will find JOY!

Whit liked my idea so much that he put JOY posters all over the soda shop to remind the kids of who really comes first. Maybe you'd like to make a JOY poster for your room, too.

Jesus
Others
Yourself

Winning Isn't Everything

Whit and Connie both noticed that Julie, a new girl in Odyssey, didn't have a partner for the three-legged race. No one chose her because everyone else had longer legs than hers. They were afraid that she'd slow her partner down.

1 John 4:7

Just then, Holly asked Julie to be her partner. "Good for her!" Connie said.

"That was an unselfish thing for Holly to do," Whit answered. "You know how much she likes to win."

"That's what's so great," Connie replied. "She gave up what *she* wanted just to help Julie feel welcome."

God wants us to help people. Sometimes that means giving up something that we want to do. And sometimes it means reaching out with love to help others.

A Little Prayer

Dear God,

Please help me to be unselfish when it comes to helping others. I don't always remember to do that. Sometimes, the things I want get in the way. But I know, Lord, that you want me to put the needs of others before my own. So that's what I'll try hard to do. Thanks for your help! Amen.

Memorize Me

Be kindly affectionate to one another with brotherly love, in honor giving preference to one another.

Romans 12:10

WORD FOR THE DAY

SACRIFICE

Sacrifice is a big word that means to give something away when you really want to keep it. Holly sacrificed winning the race just so she could help Julie feel welcome and at home. That was a very unselfish thing to do.

Sometimes you won't have to sacrifice anything to help someone. Other times you will have to choose between keeping something for yourself or helping someone else. Sometimes we sacrifice time and energy, too. A nice sacrifice to make would be sweeping an elderly neighbor's porch on a Saturday morning. It wouldn't be too hard to give up a couple cartoons to make someone else very happy!

It's easy to notice our own sacrifices. Some day, watch your mom or dad to find their sacrifices. Did they ever buy you new tennis shoes when their own sneakers looked old? Try giving up something for them one day! It will make them smile!

A Little Bit for Everyone

"What kind of fruit do you want in your lunch box?" Mrs. Taylor asked Jesse and Dylan.

"Banana!" they both answered at once.

"We only have one banana left," Mom said. "One of you will have to choose something else."

Acts 2:44-45

"I'll take the banana," Jesse answered. "It's my favorite."

"It's my favorite, too!" Dylan said. "*You* pick something else."

"Hey kids, don't fight," Mrs. Taylor said. "I have an idea about how you can share. I'll give each of you half the banana. Then you pick out some other fruit to go with it."

"Sounds good to me," Dylan said.

"Me, too," answered Jesse.

God wants us to share what we have with others. When we keep everything for ourselves, we are being selfish.

A Little Prayer

Dear Lord,
You've given me so many good things: my family, our home, my friends, and the food we eat. I promise to share what I have with others, because I know it's the right thing to do.
Amen.

Memorize Me

Now all who believed were together, and had all things in common, and sold their possessions and goods, and divided them among all, as anyone had need.
ACTS 2:44-45

WORD FOR THE DAY

SELFISH

Have you thought about what the word *selfish* means?

Selfish people think what they want is the most important thing of all. Selfish people don't care about pleasing God or helping other people. They only care about themselves. And selfish people don't like to share. They don't want to give anything up.

Dylan and Jesse didn't think about sharing the banana. But when they were given the idea, they both liked it. That's because Dylan and Jesse aren't selfish.

How about you? Do you like to share? You know, if you ever meet someone selfish, share something with him or her. You'll help teach by your example!

Holly's Sacrifice

"I found twenty dollars," Holly told Whit. "Can I keep it?"

"We have to try to find out who it belongs to," Whit said.

"But if we can't, then I can keep it, right?"

Matthew 5:42

"Then it's yours," Whit answered. "Would you do me a favor?"

"Sure, Mr. Whittaker," Holly said.

"There was a fire in Connellsville. A family lost their home and they need clothing. Will you ask your mother if she can spare any?"

"Sure, Mr. Whittaker," Holly said. "And take my twenty dollars. If nobody claims it, then give it to those people."

God wants us to think less about what we want and more about what others need.

A Little Prayer

Dear Lord,
Thank you for my family, my home, and my friends. Thank you for providing for all of my needs. Help me to see what others need and to share the things I have.
Amen.

WORD FOR THE DAY

GiVE

Give is a simple little word, but the act of giving is very powerful. When we give to someone, God sees. And our giving makes Him very happy.

Memorize Me

"And whoever compels you to go one mile, go with him two. Give to him who asks you, and from him who wants to borrow from you do not turn away."
MATTHEW 5:41–42

DID YOU KNOW?

GIVE TO OTHERS

Holly could have bought something with the twenty dollars, but instead, she gave it away. And that was a good thing to do. Did you know that God wants us to be the best we can be? That means being unselfish with everything we have.

There are people all over the world who need things. Some of them are in your hometown, some are right here in Odyssey, and some are in other countries. Sometimes I notice what people need is just a smile—or a pat on the back. Those ways to give might be the easiest, but those needs can be difficult to see.

Keep your eyes open for those who are in need. You might be able to help them by giving them food or clothing. Or just a big smile! God wants us to help others, and helping others is a wonderful way to be unselfish.

Kids Are Important

Matthew 18:1–5

"You'll have to leave," Eugene said. "It's dangerous in the lab today. You'll understand when–"

"I'm older," Dylan finished.

"Eugene just wants you to be safe," Whit said. "He doesn't mean to make you feel unimportant or too little to help."

"Yeah, I know," said Dylan. "It's okay."

"That makes me happy, Dylan," Whit said with a grin. "I can tell you that Jesus thinks you're at a very special, important age.

"Jesus said that people who are humble, like children, will be the greatest in the kingdom of heaven."

Tiny children never notice when a person is wealthy, poor, beautiful, or ugly. Jesus doesn't want us to notice, either. He wants us to love each other no matter how little or big or what we are.

A Little Prayer

Dear Jesus,
There are so many things that kids can't do. So, I'm glad that you think I'm important. But help me to be humble. Let me see all your children as you do—equal to one another. Thank you for loving me so much and for watching over me. Help me to be patient, Lord. It's hard being little sometimes. Amen.

Memorize Me

"Therefore whoever humbles himself as this little child is the greatest in the kingdom of heaven."
MATTHEW 18:4

WORD FOR THE DAY

HUMBLE

Here's another word that you should know. It's the word humble. Humble people don't think that they're more important than other people.

It's fun to win a race or a contest, isn't it? But it doesn't matter to God which of us is the fastest or the smartest. You know, though, God does want us to be humble, like when we were tiny children.

Really little children—toddlers, especially—can be very *humble*. They don't care if other people are pretty, if they have a lot of things, or if they are good (or bad!) at doing something.

Jesus says that everyone should be humble like a little child. Jesus loves children and He thinks that they are *very* important.

It All Takes Time

DEVOTION

"Have you always been an inventor?" Holly asked.

"Well, Holly, I've always been interested in new ideas, but I've had lots of different jobs," Whit answered.

Psalm 40:1

"I don't know what I want to be yet," Holly told him. "I can't make up my mind."

"You'll just have to wait and see," Whit replied, smiling at his friend.

"I hate waiting," Holly said.

"Waiting can be hard to do, Holly, but God uses patience to help our faith grow."

There are many times in life when we have to wait. But God is always there waiting with us. And if we believe in Him and trust Him, we'll learn a lot while we're waiting.

✦ A Little Prayer ✦

Dear Jesus,
Please help me to be patient. Waiting is hard.
But I'm glad that you're here waiting with me.
Amen.

WORD FOR THE DAY

PATiENCE

Patience is what you have when you wait for something without getting upset. Like when you have to wait in line at the slide or swings. You don't get mad or fussy because it isn't your turn yet. You just wait with patience.

Memorize Me

"I waited patiently for the Lord; And He inclined to me, And heard my cry."
PSALM 40:1

WHIT'S CORNER

Being Patient

I sure know that it isn't always easy to have patience. So when I have trouble being patient, I just think about Job, from the Old Testament in the Bible. Job had a good relationship with God. And God blessed him and his family. But then Job lost everything. His children were killed. He lost his money and became poor. Then he got sick.

JOB 40–42

Job didn't understand why these terrible things had happened to him. He asked God about it, but God didn't explain it to him. God was upset that Job didn't trust Him. And God expected Job to be patient and wait with trust in Him.

Well, after awhile Job was sorry he hadn't trusted God, and he prayed to him. God forgave Job and blessed him again. The Bible says he gave Job twice as much as he'd owned before. His brothers and sisters came to visit him. And his friends even brought him gifts.

God took care of Job, and he'll take care of you, too. All you have to do is trust him.

Telling the Truth

"Something weird happened at school today," Jesse said to Connie.

Colossians 3:9–10

"What?" Connie asked.

"I saw Stephanie stealing money from the pockets of the kids' coats. I don't think she saw me though."

"Did you tell somebody about it?" Connie wondered.

"No," Jesse said. "I didn't want to be a tattletale. I wasn't sure what to do."

Sometimes it's hard to know what to do when you see someone do something wrong. If you're not sure about what to do, ask a grownup. Our parents and ministers want to know when we see something wrong happening. Always remember that God wants you to be truthful about anything you say.

A Little Prayer

Dear God,

Sometimes I don't know what to do when I see someone doing the wrong thing. I want to be honest. So, please help me to know when it is right to tell and when it is right to be quiet. Especially help me if I think someone could get in trouble. The Bible tells me not to steal, but other kids might not know this. Please help me remember not to be afraid.

Thank you for teaching me what is right and what is wrong. I want to pray that others will learn this, too.

Amen.

Memorize Me

You shall not steal, nor deal falsely, nor lie to one another.
LEVITICUS 19:11

WORD FOR THE DAY

HONEST

If you're *honest,* it means that you tell the truth. It means that people can trust you. God wants us to be like He is, and God is always honest. The Bible says that God cannot lie. So, we shouldn't lie either.

Sometimes it's hard to know when it's right to be honest. Jesse worried about being a tattletale when she saw someone stealing. But if you see something bad happen, and you don't tell someone about it, then you're not being honest. But when you tell, be careful about **who** you tell. You can trust your parents, because they usually know just what to do. And always remember that it's okay to remind other people to be honest.

Honesty

DEVOTION

"Eugene!" Connie cried. "What happened in here? The lab is a mess."

"You are witnessing creativity at work," Eugene answered.

"There's yucky stuff all over the place! It looks like something blew up," Connie said.

Proverbs 12:17,19,20,22

Eugene began to blush. "Well, actually, it was an experiment that went wrong," he said.

"Well, why didn't you just say so?" Connie asked.

God wants us always to tell the truth. Sometimes we get embarrassed about mistakes we make, and it's hard to admit them. Remember that hiding the truth is dishonest, even if you try to hide it with a joke!

A Little Prayer

Dear God,

I want to be truthful, even when I am embarrassed or afraid to say what's happening. Help me remember that hiding the truth is sometimes like lying. And please forgive me when I don't tell the truth, and help me not to lie again.

Amen.

WORD FOR THE DAY

TRUTH

The truth is what is real or factual. Jesus says the truth sets us free. And the Bible says that Jesus is the truth. When we tell the truth, we become a little bit more like Jesus.

Memorize Me

"And you shall know the truth, and the truth shall make you free."

JOHN 8:32

DID YOU KNOW?

ABRAHAM AND SARAH

Did you know that even a little lie can cause great harm or danger?

Genesis 20

In the Bible, a husband named Abraham and his wife, Sarah, traveled to a place called Gerar. Abraham didn't know anyone there, and he was afraid that someone might take Sarah away from him. So he lied. He said that Sarah was his sister. But then, things backfired. That one little lie caused a lot of pain and suffering for innocent people. In fact, a king almost died because of Abraham's lie.

Lying is never the right thing to do—not even if you're embarrassed or afraid. I was embarrassed when Connie saw my enormous mess in the laboratory. But Connie is my friend—I should have revealed what had happened. It's always best to tell the truth.

Asking for Help

Psalm 28:7

"Mr. Whittaker," Dylan said. "I have a problem."

"What is it?" Whit asked.

"It's Jesse. She won't leave me alone. She follows me everywhere!"

"That's because she looks up to you, Dylan. You're her big brother."

"I know," Dylan answered. "I should be patient with her. But sometimes I just want to be alone with my friends."

"Have you talked to her about it?" Whit asked.

"Yeah, but she doesn't get it," Dylan said.

"Why don't you ask God for help?" Whit suggested. "He'll give you the wisdom to do what's right."

It's good to ask other people to help you. But God wants you to remember to ask for His help first.

A Little Prayer

Dear God,
Sometimes I try to do things all by myself, and I forget that you want to help me. Please remind me to talk to you first. It'll be easier to solve my problems that way.
Amen.

WORD FOR THE DAY

SHiELD

A shield is something that protects people. In Bible times, soldiers held shields to protect themselves from weapons—like spears. The Bible says that the Lord is our shield. That means that God will protect us when things go wrong.

DID YOU KNOW?

GOD WANTS TO HELP YOU

Did you know that Whit tells great stories? Here's one he told Dylan:

There was a boy who tried to move a big stone. As hard as he tried, he couldn't do it. His father was watching him. "Are you trying as hard as you can?"

"Yes," the boy answered. "But I can't do it!"

"There's one thing you haven't done."

"What, Dad?" he asked. "I thought I tried everything."

"You haven't asked me for help."

Whit told Dylan that story to remind him to ask his heavenly Father for help. It's important to talk to God first whenever you have a problem.

Ask God For Help

DEVOTION

"Eugene," Whit said. "You've been working hard. Why don't you take a break?"

Psalm 91

"Not yet," Eugene answered. "I'm trying to improve the power source for the Strata-Flyer. This equation should help, but I can't understand it."

Whit looked at the letters and numbers Eugene was reading. "This is complicated," Whit said. "It may be beyond what we can understand."

"What do you suggest?" Eugene asked.

"We'll keep trying to figure it out," he answered. "And we'll pray and ask God to help our understanding."

Go to God with all of your problems—none are too big or too small. Try it!

A Little Prayer

Dear God,

Whenever I have a problem, whether little or big, I will ask you to be my helper. Please help me remember to pray when there's no way I can figure out the answer.

Amen.

WORD FOR THE DAY

DELIVER

The word *deliver* can mean different things. One of the meanings is "to set free." The Bible says that God will deliver us from evil. That means that when we trust Him, he will set us free from harmful things.

Memorize Me

He shall call upon Me, and I will answer him; I will be with him in trouble; I will deliver him and honor him.
PSALM 91:15

DID YOU KNOW?

GOD WILL HELP YOU!

Whenever something goes wrong in the laboratory, I always know Mr. Whittaker will help me.

I'm sure you have people to assist you, too. Whenever you have a problem that's too complicated to solve, it's reassuring to know that other people can help. I often find great satisfaction in helping others.

Did you know that God is the greatest helper there is? You can call on Him any time to ask for His help. He always hears and answers our prayers. Even when we don't understand his answer, He always does what's best for us.

So remember, no matter how great your problem is, God will never let you down. He loves you, and there's no problem He can't solve.

Sometimes Bad Things Happen

"Mr. Whittaker, I'm so sad about my friend whose grandpa died," Carter said. "How can God let bad things happen?"

Psalm 112:7

"We don't always understand the things He does," Whit said. "But we do know that everything is a part of His plan. And we know He loves us."

"But bad things make me sad," Carter answered. "And my friend's sadder than me."

"I know," Whit said. "It makes me very sad, too."

God knows that we don't always understand why things happen the way they do. He wants us to trust Him so that our hearts will be strong when times are hard.

A Little Prayer

Dear God,
When bad things happen, I will remember that everything is a part of your plan. Help me to remember this. I believe that you always do what's best and that you always love me.
Amen.

WORD FOR THE DAY

ENDURE

Endure means "to last." We want good things to last a long time so that we can enjoy them. Psalm 136:1 says that the Lord's mercy endures forever. That means that God's forgiving kindness will last for all time. That's forever!

> ## Memorize Me!
> Oh, give thanks to the Lord, for He is good! For His mercy endures forever.
> PSALM 136:1

DiD YoU KNOW?

WHEN YOU'RE SAD

I suppose I could try to invent something that would stop bad things from happening. But there isn't an inventor on Earth who can do such a thing. So when sad times come, we have to trust in the Lord.

It's easy to know that God loves you when things are going well. But when things go wrong, do you feel like blaming God or do you ever doubt His love?

The Bible says that God's mercy lasts forever. That means that He will be kind and loving toward you, even when bad things happen. Whenever you feel sad, tell God about it. He loves you very much, and he can help you through it.

Going Swimming

Phillipians 4:19

Sal watched Whit and Dylan packing for their trip to the lake. "I want to go swimming, too," Sal said softly wiping his eyes.

"You can go next time," Whit said. "You've had an ear infection, and your mom doesn't think you should swim."

"She doesn't understand that I really, really want to go swimming," Sal answered.

"I know it seems like that," Whit answered. "But she's watching out for you, and she knows what you need to do."

"Maybe you're right," said Sal.

"Do you know that God watches out for you, too?" Whit asked. "Just like your mom, God knows what's best. And He always gives you exactly what you need."

When you ask God for something, He might say "no." You shouldn't feel angry when that happens, because God always knows what you need.

A Little Prayer

Dear God,
I know that sometimes I ask you for selfish things. Sometimes it's hard for me to see the difference between what I think I want and what I really need. Please help me understand this difference. Thank you for knowing what's best for me. You always give me just what I need.
Amen.

Memorize Me

"Ask, and it will be given to you; seek, and you will find; knock, and it will be opened to you."
MATTHEW 7:7

WORD FOR THE DAY

NEED

Sal really wanted to go swimming, but he didn't **need** to. The things we **need** are always good for us. The things we want might or might not be good.

You need food and clothes and a place to live. You need air to breathe and water to drink.

You don't need candy and toys. You don't need to stay up late. You don't need to do everything that your friends do.

I try to ask myself questions to tell the difference between wants and needs. Like, sometimes when I get home from work, I'm all dirty and so tired. I really don't **want** to take a bath. But I ask myself, "What do I really need?" Then I jump into the shower, because it's what I **need** to do.

God is like a parent. He knows what you need, and He knows what you want. When you ask Him for something, He'll decide what's best. And He'll give you whatever you need.

God Is Everywhere

Connie and Holly were eating pizza together when Holly thought that she heard Connie whisper something. "What did you say?" Holly asked. But Connie didn't answer her. "Connie?"

Psalm 55:17

"I'm sorry, Holly. Did you say something?" Connie wondered.

"I heard you whispering," Holly said. "Were you talking to me?"

"No, Holly. I was talking to God," Connie answered.

"While you're eating?"

Connie laughed. "Sure. Don't you know that God is everywhere? You can pray to Him no matter what you're doing."

DEVOTION

God is everywhere. You can talk to him any time and any place. He will always hear you.

A Little Prayer

Dear God,

I don't understand how you can be everywhere at the same time, but that's okay. It's one of those great things about you that is too wonderful to understand. Thank you for being with me everywhere I go. And thank you for helping me all through the day.

Please help me remember to talk to you anytime. I forget to say grace at school sometimes, but I want to remember! When this happens, give me the courage to just say my thanks. I want to thank you—and praise you—no matter who is around. Amen.

WORD FOR THE DAY

OMNIPRESENT

Eugene likes big words, and this is one of his favorites. Omnipresent means "everywhere." God is everywhere, so God is omnipresent. When you're at school, God is with you. If you're playing with your friends, God is there too. He's with you when you're sleeping. He's there when you wake up.

You don't have to be lonely, because God is omnipresent. Wherever you are, that's where God is. I think that's great; don't you?

Why don't you try out this big word on other people? If they don't know what it means, you can share this word!

Vocabulary
Listen
Human
Omnipresent
Cheer

Memorize Me

Evening and morning and at noon
I will pray, and cry aloud,
And He shall hear my voice.
Psalm 55:17

DEVOTION

Remember to Say Thank You

Luke 17:11-19

"Wow!" said Dylan. "That was cool. Did you see how awesome Odyssey looked from way up there?"

"Yeah," Sal answered. "I can't believe that Mr. Whittaker took us for a ride in the Strata-Flyer. I can't wait to tell Carter about it."

"Uh-oh," Dylan said. "I think we forgot something."

"What?" asked Sal.

"We didn't thank Mr. Whittaker."

"You're right," Sal said. "Let's go back and thank him."

Do you sometimes forget to say thank you? When you let people know that you appreciate them, it makes them happy.

A Little Prayer

Dear God,

Thank you for this day. I appreciate everything you give me. Most of all, thank you for those gifts you give that I can't see—your protection, your help, and your Son, Jesus Christ. Thanks for everything!

Amen.

WORD FOR THE DAY

COURTS

In Bible times, many leaders lived in fancy places called *courts*. When the Bible says, "Come into His courts with praise," it means to praise the Lord when you come to him in prayer.

Memorize Me

Enter into His gates with thanksgiving,
And into His courts with praise.
Be thankful to Him, and bless His name.
PSALM 100:4

DID YOU KNOW?

GOD LOVES TO BE THANKED

Although there are always reasons to give God thanks, you don't need a special occasion to do so. When the Bible says to give thanks to the Lord, it doesn't mean that you have to wait for Him to do something special for you. There are countless things to thank Him for each day.

You can thank God for your family, your friends, pets, health, happiness—almost anything you can think of. God gives you these special blessings every day. We usually remember to thank God at bedtime—but it's good to thank him any time.

Sometimes I talk to Him when I'm alone in the laboratory at Whit's End. You can thank Him wherever you are, and you can be sure that God will always hear you.

A Surprise for Eugene

DEVOTION

"Eugene," Whit said. "I have something for you to do."

"Yes?" Eugene asked.

Luke 11:5–13

"Well, for weeks now, you've been asking if you can try out the new hydroxide accelerator on the Strata-Flyer. Well, today is the day."

"Why, Mr. Whittaker!" squeaked Eugene. "Please accept my authenticated gratitude."

"Accepted," said Whit. "You've really studied, worked, and tested until you were ready, so let's go for a ride."

When we work hard for what's important to us, eventually God rewards us. He knows when we're ready!

A Little Prayer

Dear God,
There's so much I want to pray for, but you are the only One who knows when I'm ready for those things. Thanks for knowing this even when I don't. And please help me to be patient when you want me to wait.
Amen.

WORD FOR THE DAY

DESIRE

When you desire something, you really want it. When your desire is for a good thing, and you keep asking God for it, He will answer your prayers. But remember—He will only give you what He knows is best for you.

Memorize Me

"If you abide in Me, and My words abide in you, you will ask what you desire, and it shall be done for you." JOHN 15:7

DID YOU KNOW?

KEEP ON ASKING GOD

I was pleased when Mr. Whittaker asked me to test fly the Strata-Flyer. It was something I had desired to do for a very long time. I'm glad that I kept asking. I knew that I could perform well. But I had to wait until Whit believed that I was completely prepared.

Prayer is much the same. If you ask God for something you want, and nothing happens, keep on asking. God might surprise you.

It's not that God doesn't want to grant you good things, or that He can't make up His mind. He merely wants to teach you to keep on praying.

We All Make Mistakes

Romans 3:23

"Look what I made!" Dylan shouted. He threw his red-winged contraption into the air, but it crashed down to the floor. "It was supposed to fly," he said.

"That's the beginning of a wonderful invention, Dylan," Whit said. "Keep at it. But did you know that the parts you used belong to Eugene and that he's been looking for them?"

"No," Dylan answered. "I thought they were just spare parts. Do you think Eugene will be mad at me?"

"You made a mistake, Dylan," said Whit. "I'm sure Eugene will forgive you."

"I am sorry," Dylan said, adding, "so I'll go apologize to Eugene right now!"

We all make mistakes. But God never wants us to give up trying to do what is right.

A Little Prayer

Dear God,

I make mistakes sometimes. I don't mean to sin, but I do it without thinking. Thank you for your forgiveness, Lord. I always know you'll still love me—even when I have sinned. Please help me to keep trying to do what's right. And help me to talk to you first when I can't decide what's right or wrong.

Amen.

Memorize Me

" . . . for all have sinned and fall short of the glory of God."
ROMANS 3:23

WORD FOR THE DAY

MISTAKE

A *mistake* is when we do something wrong because we aren't thinking clearly. Sometimes, a mistake causes us to sin. Dylan was so excited about building his flying machine that he took Eugene's things without asking. That was the wrong thing to do. But it really was a mistake.

It's important to know, though, that all mistakes are not sins! We all have accidents. The other day, I broke a dish at Whit's End. That was just a mistake. Now, if I hadn't told Whit about it—*that* would have been sinful.

God knows that everyone makes mistakes. He also knows that everyone sins. He'll forgive us when we ask Him to.

Most of all, God wants you to keep on trying to make good choices. The best way to do that is to remember to put Him first. If there's something that you're not sure of, think about what God would do. Trust Him to help you.

What's Temptation?

And lead us not into temptation. Dylan said those words every time he prayed the Lord's Prayer. He decided to ask Whit what they meant.

Luke 11:4

"Well, Dylan," Whit said, "Temptation is when you want to do something that you know is wrong. So the words mean "help us to not want to do wrong things." Whit smiled.

"You know Dylan, God has rules for us to follow. They help keep us safe and from doing what's wrong. When you read your Bible and think about what it says, you'll understand better how to do the *right* thing."

The Bible is filled with good rules that God made for us. They help us know right from wrong.

✦ A Little Prayer ✦

Dear God,
Thank you for giving us the Ten Commandments. I don't understand all of them yet, but I will try to obey your laws. Amen.

WORD FOR THE DAY

COMMANDMENT

A *commandment* is an order. It isn't something that someone asks you to do. It's something that someone demands that you do. So it's very important that we follow God's commandments.

Memorize Me

And do not lead us into temptation, But deliver us from the evil one.
LUKE 11:4

WHIT'S  CORNER

The Ten Commandments

Every family has rules to follow. We try hard to remember and obey them. Rules like, "don't cross the street by yourself" and "never talk to strangers" help keep us safe. Our parents made these rules because they love us.

DEUTERONOMY 5

Well, you know that God loves you, too. He also wants you to be safe. And He knows it's important to be nice to other people. That's why He gave us a special set of rules. They're called the Ten Commandments.

Do you know what the Ten Commandments are? You can find them in your Bible. Just look in Exodus 20:1-20 or Deuteronomy 5:1-22.

FUN To Do:

Use colored pencils or crayons to make your own list of the Ten Commandments. You can hang them on your wall, and each day, you'll be reminded of how God wants you to behave.

You shall have no other gods before Me

You shall not make and bow down to a carved image, or any likeness of anything.

You shall not take the name of the Lord in vain

Remember the Sabbath days to keep it holy

Honor your father and your mother.

Asking for Forgiveness

Psalm 51:1–10

Jesse and her friends were playing dress up one afternoon. Jesse got some clothes from her mother's closet. She even took out her Mom's very best blue dress.

"I'm going to wear this one," Jesse said. Then she put on the pretty dress. But while they were playing, an awful thing happened. The blue dress tore!

"What are you going to do now?" Sarah cried. "Your mom's going to be so mad!"

"This is all my fault," said Jesse. "I really shouldn't have taken her clothes without asking. I'm gonna go tell her I'm so sorry right away."

God wants you to be honest about your mistakes, and He wants you to apologize when you do something wrong.

A Little Prayer

Dear God,

I'm so glad you forgive my sins, Lord. Thank you for having love that never changes no matter what I do. But, when I do something wrong, whether I mean to or not, I want you to help me remember to say I'm sorry.

Sometimes it's scary to tell people when I've messed something up. Help me to not be afraid. I always want to be honest about my mistakes and sins. And I always want to apologize.

Not only to other people, God, but to you, too! I am truly sorry for my sins, God. Please forgive me.

Amen.

WORD FOR THE DAY

APOLOGiZE

Do you always apologize when you do something wrong? To apologize means to say that you're sorry. You can also say, "I apologize."

God wants you to apologize to the people you've hurt. He wants you to say "I'm sorry," and ask for their forgiveness. That's what Jesse did. She told her mom about the dress, and she said she was sorry.

When you do something wrong, you should apologize to God, too. That's because when you sin, you are breaking God's rules. He feels bad when you don't behave in good ways. But the good news is that God forgives you when you ask Him to!

Memorize Me

Create in me a clean heart, O God, And renew a steadfast spirit within me.
Psalm 51:10

Great Job, Connie!

DEVOTION

Whit decided to have something cold to drink.

Matthew 23:11-12

"How about a lemonade, please?" he asked Connie with smile.

"Coming right up," Connie answered.

"How's your volunteer work going at Bible Camp?" Whit asked.

Connie smiled. "It's going fine. But all I ever do is read stories to the kids and help clean up. It's really no big deal."

"Oh, but it is, Connie," said Whit. "The Bible says that great people aren't the ones who are served. Great people are the ones who serve others— and your work at camp makes you a very special servant."

It isn't being powerful or important that makes a person great. Greatness comes from helping others.

A Little Prayer

Dear God,

Thank you for sending the best servant ever—your Son—to Earth. He helped us all. I want to be a good servant, too.

You help me all the time, so I want to be a good helper to you, too. Sometimes I don't notice when people need help. Please help me see when I'm needed—and please give me the patience and time to help out. I promise to try to help other people whenever I can.

Amen.

Memorize Me

"And whoever exalts himself will be humbled, and he who humbles himself will be exalted."
MATTHEW 23:12

WORD FOR THE DAY

SERVANT

A *servant* is a helper—someone who *serves,* or does things for other people. People serve each other all the time by helping or caring for each other. God wants you to be a good helper to everyone, not because you have to, but because you want to.

You already know that I love serving. I help at Bible Camp, with Sunday School classes, and at vacation Bible school. God loves it when I serve people by teaching about Him!

Think about ways you can serve others. Maybe you could help your sister or brother learn a Bible verse from this book. Or maybe you'd like to help a neighbor with some work.

God loves His servants!

Jesus Understands

"You're so quiet, Carter," Whit said.

"I feel bad," Carter said. "I almost stole Sal's trading card."

"Almost?" Whit asked.

"It was the coolest card! I really wanted it and thought about taking it, but I didn't do it."

Hebrews 4:14–16

"You did the right thing," said Whit.

"But I wanted to, and that's bad!"

"All of us have bad thoughts," Whit explained. "Even Jesus was tempted. But you stayed strong, Carter. It would have been wrong if you had given in to your feelings."

Jesus faced temptation, but He never gave in. If you feel like doing something wrong, remember Jesus understands this feeling. Ask Him, and He will help you to be strong.

A Little Prayer

Dear Jesus,
Sometimes I think about doing wrong things.
Thank you for loving me even if sometimes my
thoughts are bad. Please stay close in my heart
to keep me standing strong!
Amen

WORD FOR THE DAY

DEED

Deed means "something that you
do." When the Bible talks about
deeds, it does mean things you do,
but it also includes what you say.

Memorize Me

And whatever you do in word or
deed, do all in the name of the
Lord Jesus, giving thanks to God
the Father through Him.
COLOSSIANS 3:17

WHIT'S  CORNER

The Source of Faith

Have you ever watched a big tree—like an oak—during a storm? The wind blows and rain pours, but the tree keeps

COLOSSIANS 2:6–7

standing. It may sway a bit, but strong roots keep it from falling—even when the storm is bad.

Jesus does the same for us. The Bible says we're like trees. And we must go through storms, too. Only our storms are on the inside—like when Carter made his choice between right and wrong.

When we ask Jesus to help us, it's easier to do the right thing. It's like building strong roots in our faith. Jesus helps us stand straight in the storm.

FUN TO DO:

Draw a picture of a squirrel planting an acorn. Then imagine that acorn growing up into a giant oak. Now draw another picture of the grown tree, a giant home for many squirrels! During the wind and rain that tree will stand straight and tall. When bad times come, ask Jesus to help, and you will be just like that oak tree.

How Long Is Forever?

"Everything *mus*t be measured," Eugene said. "Everything has a beginning and an end!"

John 6:47

"Not forever," Connie argued. "It doesn't matter how long *forever* is, anyway. What matters is that it's God's promise."

"What are you two talking about?" Whit asked.

"Eternal life," Connie answered. "Jesus promised that if we believe in Him, our spirits will live forever in heaven. But Genius here is more concerned about how *long* forever is."

Whit chuckled. "Well, Eugene," he said. "Forever has no beginning and no end. But since you believe in Jesus, you'll have plenty of time to figure it out."

Jesus said that if you trust Him as your Savior, your soul will live forever. Is Jesus Christ your Savior?

A Little Prayer

Dear Jesus,

Thank you for your gift of eternal life. I know that you died on the cross for our sins, and that you live again so we can live forever.

I believe in you, Jesus, and I accept you as my Savior.

Amen

WORD FOR THE DAY

EVERLASTING

"Ever" means "always," and "lasting" means "going on." So the word *everlasting* means "always going on"—or, in other words, forever!

DID YOU KNOW?

Jesus promises that if we believe in Him and trust Him to be our Savior, our spirits will live forever with Him in heaven. Did you know that's what eternal life means—to live forever?

I still have trouble contemplating *forever*, but I do understand eternal life. Someday our bodies will get old and die. This invariably happens to all humans. But Jesus says that who we really are on the inside—our spirits—can go on living, even though our bodies have died.

Do you know Jesus as your Savior? He wants us to understand that He died for our sins to give us eternal life. He wants to be our Savior so we can all live with him forever. However long that is!

belief = eternal life

Who Do You Want to Be Like?

"When I grow up, I want to be just like Mr. Whittaker," Dylan said.

"Why is that?" asked his mom.

"Because he's awesome. He can do just about anything!"

Luke 6:40

"That's true," Mrs. Taylor answered. "But you don't have to wait until you're grown to be like him."

"I don't?" Dylan said.

"Mr. Whittaker tries to behave like Jesus in everything he does," his mom said. "And that makes him the kind of person he is. If you try to behave like Jesus, then you'll be like Whit, too."

No matter how old or young we might be, we can always try to behave like Jesus.

⋆ A Little Prayer ⋆

Dear Jesus,
It makes me feel safe—knowing that if I follow your Word, you will think that I am wise. Please help me to be like you.
Amen

WORD FOR THE **DAY**

FOUNDATION

A good foundation is what makes a building strong. It's the part at the bottom of a house—often made of concrete blocks with big steel bars that go deeply into the ground. Jesus is the foundation of our faith. Our belief and trust in Him is the "rock" we build on that makes us strong Christians.

Memorize Me!

"Therefore whoever hears these sayings of Mine, and does them, I will liken him to a wise man who built his house on the rock."
MATTHEW 7:24

WHIT'S CORNER

A Solid Foundation

Have you ever taken a good look at Whit's End? It's built on solid rock, a firm foundation that was here **MATTHEW 7:24–29** before anyone even thought of Whit's End. A long, long time ago, the same foundation was used for a church, the mayor's house, and then later, a community center. Now that's a strong foundation!

Jesus talks about foundations in the Bible. He says that wise people build their homes on a rock-solid foundation. Those houses will stand strong. But foolish people build their houses on sand. And when a big storm comes, their houses are washed away.

He's telling us that we are like houses—strong or weak, depending on how we're built. Jesus wants us to be strong. He's like the rock beneath our houses. When we build our lives on Him, we'll stand strong, no matter what happens.

A New Kid in School

DEVOTION

"Connie," Dylan said. "Has anyone ever picked on you?"

"Sure," Connie answered. "Why?"

"There's this new kid in school, and nobody likes him. He calls us names and stuff."

John 13:34

"I don't know what to say, Dylan, except that God says you have to love him."

"Love him!" Dylan cried. "How can I love him when he's mean to everybody?"

"We can still love even when people aren't being nice," Connie said. "Try to get to know him better. Maybe you can play ball with him and introduce him to your friends."

God wants us to love everyone. Even people we don't know or don't like.

A Little Prayer

Dear Jesus,

You know it's hard for me to like some people. But I know that you want me to love one another. So please help me to be kind and loving to everyone, even the people I don't like.

Amen

WORD FOR THE DAY

COMPASSIONATE

Are you a *compassionate* person? This is a big word that means "kind and forgiving." Being compassionate is one way that we can love one another. And remember—God wants you to be kind and forgiving to everyone.

Memorize Me

"A new command I give to you, that you love one another."
JOHN 13:34

DiD YOU KNOW?

Did you know that Jesus says we should love one another the way He loves us? When you think of how much Jesus loves us, this seems virtually impossible.

Thankfully, Jesus doesn't give us rules that are impossible to obey. In this case, when Jesus says "love," he doesn't mean our warm and fuzzy feelings. Instead, He means that we should be compassionate to one another.

If you make the choice to be kind and forgiving to others—even if you don't feel like it—you could surprise yourself! Maybe you'll discover that you actually do love the people that you thought you didn't like!

What Friends Are

"Eugene, do you know what I like best of all about Whit's End?" asked Mr. Whittaker.

John 15:14

"Maybe it's historical significance?" Eugene offered.

"No," Whit chuckled. "My favorite thing is enjoying my friends who come here—you, Connie, Sal, Carter, Holly, Dylan, everybody. That's what I like most."

"You're right," Eugene said. "Seeing our friends and being with them is the best."

Whit smiled. "The Bible says there's a friend that sticks closer than a brother—God."

Friends are a gift from God. And His greatest gift—our very best friend—is Jesus. Remember to thank God for all His wonderful gifts.

★ A Little Prayer ★

Dear God,

I'm so glad that we're friends! Thank you for your Son, who is my best friend. And thank you for sending me all my friends who are people. You are such a good friend, Lord! I want to be a good friend, too. Not only to you and Jesus, but to everyone around me. Please give me a hand with that!

Amen

WORD FOR THE DAY

FRIEND

You know what a *friend* is. But do you know how to be a good friend? Proverbs 17:17 says that a friend loves at all times. That means that you should love your friends even when they do things that you don't like. How about it? Do you love your friends all the time?

DID YOU KNOW?

Just as Mr. Whittaker says, God does give us friends. But God gives us His friendship, too. Did you know that He is always there whenever you need Him? Even though you can't see Him, God sees you. He always listens, and He always cares. No matter what you do, God will love you. And there's nothing you can do that He won't forgive.

God's special friendship shows us how to be friends with others. Remember to be a good listener. Try to be there for your friends when they need you. And show your forgiveness easily and swiftly.

As with other friendships, God wants you to spend time with Him . . . that's a wonderful way to become better friends with Him.

Memorize Me

And he was called the friend of God.
JAMES 2:23

The Spelling Bee

Dylan was alone when he came to Whit's End.

James 3:16

"Where's your buddy Sal?" asked Whit.

"He won the spelling bee again," Dylan answered with a scowl. "He's having cake at his house."

"You sound a little jealous," Whit said.

"I am," Dylan answered. "I only came in third."

"But Sal is your friend," Whit smiled. "And a friend loves at all times. We all have talents, Dylan. Wouldn't it get boring if they were all the same?"

"Yeah, I guess you're right," Dylan admitted. "And I don't like being bored. I'm gonna go over to Sal's and tell him I'm proud of him!"

God doesn't want us to be jealous of other people. He made all of us just the way He wants us to be—we're all winners!

A Little Prayer

Dear God,
Sometimes I see the things that my friends have, and I want those things, too. And sometimes I see someone who is popular or good looking, and I want to be like him or her. I don't want to be a jealous friend. You made me just the way you wanted to, Lord—and I need your help to always remember this! I praise you for making me and providing for me. Thank you for everything, God.
Amen

Memorize Me

For where envy and self-seeking exist, confusion and every evil thing are there.
James 3:16

WORD FOR THE DAY

JEALOUS

The word *jealous* means "to envy." And that means to want something that somebody else already has.

Have you ever been jealous? I have. I'm sometimes jealous of Eugene, because he's so smart. (Please don't tell him I said that.)

It's never right to be jealous. The Bible says that where there's jealousy there's confusion and evil. We don't want to be confused. And we sure don't want to be evil. Whenever I feel jealousy, I ask God to help me let go of that feeling.

So, try to be thankful for what you have. If someone you know has nicer

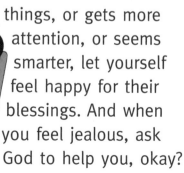

things, or gets more attention, or seems smarter, let yourself feel happy for their blessings. And when you feel jealous, ask God to help you, okay?

Trusting Friends

DEVOTION

Holly came to Whit's End carrying her cat, Jasper. "Poor kitty," she said. "You had such a bad weekend."

Philippians 4:8

Dylan overheard. "Cats can't have bad weekends," he said.

"Well, he did," Holly answered. "While we were away, I asked my new friend Kate to feed Jasper—and she forgot!"

"Too bad," Dylan said. "You could've asked me to do it. I'm a great pet sitter."

"You know, Dylan," Holly said, "as much as Sherman doesn't like Jasper, I can trust you. Next time I'll ask you to help me."

It's important to remember to keep promises to friends. That's how we earn their trust!

A Little Prayer

Dear God,

Thank you for giving me people to trust! And thank you for trusting me, Lord, to be responsible. Please help me be trustworthy in everything I do.

Amen

WORD FOR THE DAY

RESPONSIBLE

Responsible people try to keep their promises. And they try to do things on time. We all make mistakes like Holly's friend. But what's important is that we keep trying to earn others' trust by being responsible! It can be tough, but God will help you try!

Memorize Me

"He who is faithful in what is least is faithful also in much; and he who is unjust in what is least is unjust also in much."

LUKE 16:10

WHIT'S CORNER

Being Trustworthy

I love Whit's End because of all the friends that I get to see here, but this job takes a lot of work. It can be pretty messy at times.

JEREMIAH 1

If I didn't keep the soda shop running well, it might become hard for my customers to trust me. You see, trust is something we earn by doing our jobs. Like when you make your bed and put away your toys, you're being trustworthy. You might not always feel like doing these jobs, but it's very important that you do them well.

The Bible says that stewards, or helpers, are to be faithful in all that they do. That means that we try to be trustworthy whenever others rely on us. No matter what the job, we are still stewards, and we help others when we are responsible all the time.

FUN TO DO:

What do you want to be when you grow up? Maybe a doctor or a firefighter or a teacher? Try to think of the different responsibilities these people have and how they earn our trust in their jobs. Ask your parents if you can meet one of them to see the different things they do!

Doing the Right Thing

DEVOTION

Proverbs 17:17

Connie couldn't stop thinking about a quarrel she'd had with Eugene that morning. When Whit had asked them to replace the old, shabby menus, Connie and Eugene couldn't agree on which color paper to use. Finally, just to end the argument, she'd agreed with his idea: bright green.

"It doesn't even match the room," she muttered, feeling totally cranky. Then the phone rang.

"Salutations," said Eugene cheerfully. "Could you please assist me in making pizza? I've got all your favorites, even pepperoni—but unfortunately, I am unfamiliar with the process. It is my hope that you haven't had dinner yet."

"Sure Eugene, I'll be glad to help! Be right there," Connie exclaimed, hanging up the phone with a grin.

Sometimes, being helpful is a great way to end a disagreement with a friend. Just try it!

A Little Prayer

Dear Jesus,
Thank you for always being there when I call on you. Lord, you help people all the time. And you never put yourself first. Sometimes I am angry or tired, and I don't want to help anybody do anything. Other times I'm just plain cranky. But I want to follow your example, Lord. Help me to be a good friend all the time—even when I don't feel like it.
Amen

WORD FOR THE DAY

HELPER

A *helper* is someone who helps. Most people like to be helpers. But really good helpers lend a hand even when they don't feel like it. Like when they're tired or angry.

I was mad at Eugene. But I still would have helped him make pizza, even if he hadn't gotten pepperoni. Yes, I did feel really cranky just before he called me. But that wasn't about our friendship. It was because we didn't agree on something.

You see, disagreements between friends can end as quickly as they start. God wants us to love our friends and be good helpers all the time.

Memorize Me

A friend loves at all times
PROVERBS 17:17

Three Special Things

DEVOTION

"May I borrow your pen, Whit?" Connie asked.

"Sure," Whit said. "What are you doing?"

Micah 6:8

"I'm making a list for my Bible study class," Connie told him. "It's a list of things God wants us to do. Do you have any suggestions?"

"Sure," Whit answered. "The prophet Micah said to do justly, to love mercy, and to walk humbly with your God."

"In other words," said Connie, "treat others right, always be kind, and don't think that you're better than anyone else."

"That's right," Whit answered.

"Those three things are very important to God. And they're also important for building strong friends."

God wants us to treat others the way we want to be treated. He wants us to respect one another.

A Little Prayer

Dear God,
Help me to treat others with respect. I want to treat everyone the same, Lord. And forgive me when I forget to respect others. Please help me learn to love all the people the same way that you do.
Amen

Memorize Me

And forgive us our sins
For we also forgive everyone
who is indebted to us.
LUKE 11:4

WORD FOR THE DAY

RESPECT

Do you know what it means to treat people with *respect?* Part of it means to use good manners with them. God wants us to use respect toward everyone. Here's how He explains it:

"For if there should come into your assembly a man with gold rings, in fine apparel, and there should also come in a poor man in filthy clothes, and you pay attention to the one wearing the fine clothes and say to him, 'You sit here in a good place,' and say to the poor man, 'You stand there,' or, 'Sit here at my footstool,' have you not shown partiality among yourselves, and become judges with evil thoughts?"

That passage is from James 2:2-4. Here, God's telling us that it is good to treat all of his people with the same respect—no matter who they are or what they look like. Jesus did that, and so should we!

A Birthday Present For Dylan

"Are you going to Dylan's birthday party?" Holly asked Sal.

"I'm not sure," Sal answered. "I don't have enough money to buy him a present."

Proverbs 11:25

"Dylan won't care," Holly said. "But if you want to earn some money, Mr. Whittaker is looking for someone to help him clean the workshop."

"That's great!" Sal cried. "Then I can buy that baseball glove that I've been wanting."

"I thought you were going to buy a present for Dylan," Holly said.

"Oh, you're right," Sal answered. "Dylan's birthday is more important."

It's easy to think only of yourself when there's something you really want. But Jesus wants you to put other people first.

A Little Prayer

Dear God,

I'm so glad you've given me my friends. Please help me put them first. And please help me remember the difference between what I want and need.

Amen

WORD FOR THE DAY

NEED

A need is more than a want or desire. A need is something we cannot live without—like food, water, shelter, or clothing. Sometimes it's easy to confuse the word "need" with "want." God knows our needs, and he promises to fill them if we seek him first!

DID YOU KNOW?

Do you ever watch those commercials on television—the ones that sell toys and games? Vast numbers of people watch those ads. And many of those viewers want everything they see!

Be careful about deciding what you must have. Did you know that God already knows what you want and need? He knows the difference between them. And he wants us to put others first.

So if you're not certain whether something is selfish, ask God. He will help you to make the right choice.

Memorize Me

The generous soul will be made rich,
And he who waters will also be watered himself.
PROVERBS 11:25

The Sick Kitty

Holly was sitting on the front steps. Whit went to sit with her.

"Are you crying, Holly?" he asked.

Philippians 4:6–7

"Oh, Mr. Whittaker," Holly sniffled. "Jasper is sick, and he has to stay overnight at the veterinarian."

"I'm so sorry, Holly," Whit said.

"Dr. Mulligan says he'll be fine, but I'm still very worried." Holly wiped a tear from her cheek.

"I know Dr. Mulligan," Whit said. "She's a good doctor, and she'll take care of Jasper. Do you know what else we should do?"

"No. What?" Holly asked.

"Let's say a prayer together," Mr. Whittaker said, "and ask God to be with Jasper."

Jesus said that we shouldn't worry, but that we should trust Him with our problems.

A Little Prayer

Dear God,
It's hard not to worry sometimes. Things happen that make me feel sad and afraid. But I know that you're always with me. I know that you'll help me. And I promise that I'll put my trust in you.
Amen.

Memorize Me

Be anxious for nothing, but in everything by prayer and supplication, with thanksgiving, let your requests be made known to God.
PHILIPPIANS 4:6

WORD FOR THE DAY

TRUST

The word for today is *trust*. When you trust someone, you have faith in him. The best one to trust is God. He is so strong and so good, that you can trust Him with anything.

Jesus said that we shouldn't worry about anything. If we have faith in Him and we trust Him to do what is best for us, everything will work out all right.

Holly was so worried about her cat. But Whit knew that they could trust Dr. Mulligan. All Holly needed was to be reminded to trust others, like she trusts Whit.

So it wasn't too hard for Whit to convince Holly that Jasper was in good hands. But Whit also knew that Jesus is the greatest helper that there is. And so they went to the Lord in prayer. That always makes me feel more trusting!

Oh, and by the way, Jasper is just fine.

Waiting Up

Connie took Jesse and Holly to the park. Jesse yelled, "Race you to the swings!" So everyone ran as fast as they could.

"Wait up!" Jesse soon called to her friends. "I'm too little to run as fast as you!"

2 Timothy 4:7

Holly and Connie slowed to let Jesse catch up to them. When they reached the playground, each claimed a swing, laughing and panting from their run.

Our relationship with God is a lot like running. And as our faith grows stronger, it's important for us to "wait up" for those who are "smaller":

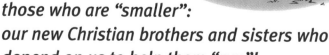

our new Christian brothers and sisters who depend on us to help them "run"!

A Little Prayer

Dear God,
Thank you for your strength! Please help me grow stronger, not just in my body, but in my faith in you.
Amen

WORD FOR THE DAY

PERSEVERE

The word *persevere* means to "keep on trying." When you're faced with problems, God doesn't want you to give up. Instead, He wants you to persevere. And that means you should keep on trying to solve your problems.

Memorize Me

Be strong and of good courage; do not be afraid, nor be dismayed, for the Lord your God is with you wherever you go.
JOSHUA 1:9

DID YOU KNOW?

Connie informs me that I should exercise my body as much as I do my brain. I'll admit I spend more time in the lab than in the gymnasium, but I am well acquainted with the benefits of exercise. Did you know the more you exercise, the stronger your body grows?

Becoming a stronger Christian works in a similar way. Whenever we encounter problems, we must work hard to overcome them. And, the more problems we overcome, the stronger our faith becomes.

Perhaps you can see your problems as God's exercise program. When you trust Him to help you, your faith will grow healthy and strong. Like my brain!

Dylan's Partner

Throughout dinner, Dylan hardly spoke. His father knew that something was wrong when Dylan said "no thanks" to dessert.

"I'm just not in the mood," he explained.

Romans 12:10

His dad said, "That's just not like you, Dylan. What's wrong?"

So Dylan explained his science project and how his class had drawn names for partners. "And I got Arnie's name," he moaned. "He's the meanest kid in school."

"I'm sorry about that," said Mr. Taylor. "You know that it's our job to be kind to each other. And usually when we try kindness, things can work out much better than we think!"

God wants us to treat everyone with brotherly love—even mean people. He tells us to do this so we can be like Him!

DiD YOU KNOW?

When Dylan and Arnie worked on their science project, they came over to the lab at Whit's End to request my assistance. I observed Dylan's kindness to Arnie while they worked. In very little time, Arnie relaxed and acted in a much more pleasant manner.

Dylan used kindness to make Arnie feel included. And it was my observation that Arnie became nicer as a result.

Do you have a classmate who is considered a bully? Did you know that God says that you should love that person even though he or she is mean? When you encounter a bully, surprise that person with kindness! That's what God wants us to do.

WORD FOR THE DAY

BULLY

A *bully* is someone who is always picking on other people. Sometimes bullies are mean to others because they think that nobody likes them. If you meet a bully, try to be kind. It's hard to be nice to someone who's mean, but that's just what Jesus would do!

A Little Prayer

Dear God,
I know kids who are bullies, and it's hard to like them. Help me remember to be kind and use brotherly love. I know that's what you want me to do.
Amen

Memorize Me

Be kindly affectionate to one another with brotherly love, in honor giving preference to one another.
ROMANS 12:10

Its Own Reward

Holly saw Dylan pushing his bike toward Whit's End.

"Hey, Holly," Dylan yelled. "Will you help me?" His bike had a flat tire, and it was hard to push.

"I'll make a deal with you," Holly said. "I'll help you if you

Philippians 2:4

help me hang curtains in my play room." Dylan thought about it. The last thing he wanted to do was hang curtains.

"I'll help you," he said. "But not in return for your help."

"What do you mean?" Holly wondered.

"Mr. Whittaker always says, 'Help each other out,'" Dylan told her. "It's what Jesus tells us to do. I'll do it just to be nice, even if you don't help me push."

We shouldn't expect something in return for helping others. Being nice is its own reward.

A Little Prayer

Dear Jesus,
Please help me watch out for what others need. And I will try to help others without expecting anything in return.
Amen

WORD FOR THE DAY

INTERESTS

The Bible says that we should look out for the *interests* of others. An *interest* is something we want to do, get, make, learn, or even say. Each person's interests are very important to him or her. Dylan needed help with his bike, and Holly needed help with her curtains. These were their interests. When you see that you can help others with one of their interests, try it.

DiD YoU KNOW?

It wasn't Holly's intention to be selfish. She merely forgot and put herself before others and God. We all make that mistake sometimes. When we're thinking about our own desires, it's easy to forget about what others might need.

Did you know that only truly selfish people make a habit of expecting something in return? Jesus doesn't want us to be like that. He wants us to help other people without thinking at all about ourselves.

So the next time you're tempted to say, "I'll do something for you, if you do something for me," think again. What would Jesus do?

Nobody's Too Little

"Connie, would you like some help?" Jesse asked.

Luke 6:40

"Sure," Connie answered. She handed Jesse a cloth.

"I don't get to help very much," Jesse said. "I'm too little for everything."

"No, you're not!" Connie said. "You may be too little for some things. But for other things, you're just right. Let's talk about what you *can* do."

We are all members of God's family. And that makes us very special. Each person has his or her own strengths or gifts—nobody is too little to help God. Use your talents to be a good helper in your school, church, and neighborhood.

A Little Prayer

Dear Lord,

Thank you for making so many special people!
Help me notice their gifts and talents.
And help me remember to tell them when
they've done something special.

Thank you especially for my church
family. Help me use the special gifts you've
given me to make your church family grow
stronger.

Amen

WORD FOR THE DAY

GIFTS

Your *gifts* are the things you do well.
Everyone has gifts. Maybe you sing
or dance. Maybe you draw very well.
Or maybe you are great at helping others.
God wants you to use your gifts—especially
in church and in Sunday School.

WHIT'S  CORNER

The Body of Christ

You know, every family is special. And each person in every family is important. Imagine how boring it would be if everyone looked and acted just the same! What do you think makes you special? Maybe you can run fast, sing songs, or draw pictures. Maybe you are nice.

1 CORINTHIANS 12:12–27

God knows everyone is special. He understands our strengths and gifts. And He wants us to help each other. God thinks of His church as one big family, and we should too—we are His children.

Jesus said to think of the church as a large body. And just like our own bodies, the church has different parts. The different parts of the

church are its members—its people. These people may be as different from one another as your toes and ears, but each one is an important part of the body. You are too! Be sure to do your best to play your part!

Give Credit Where It's Due

"Sal, this is truly amazing," said Eugene. "A perfect replica of a 1968 single-engine plane. You did a great job."

2 Chronicles 32:24–26

"Thanks, Eugene," Sal answered. "But, it's made from a kit."

"Well, you did a superb job. And it's obvious you've put a lot of work into it," Eugene said.

"Dylan helped, too," Sal answered, "so it's not just my plane. It took us a whole month to build it."

Sal did the right thing. He gave Dylan credit for helping. God wants us to thank our helpers. And we should thank God, too. He's the best helper there is.

Memorize Me

Oh come, let us sing to the LORD! Let us shout joyfully to the Rock of our salvation. Let us come before His presence with thanksgiving; Let us shout joyfully to Him with psalms.

PSALM 95:1-2

A Little Prayer

Dear God,

You do so many nice things for me. Thank you very much! And thanks for sending me help through other people! I can always count on your help, Lord. I pray for your help now—help to remember to say "thank you" to all the people who help me.

Amen

WORD FOR THE DAY

PSALMS

Psalms are like songs to the Lord. The Book of Psalms, in the Bible, is a collection of prayers, poems, and hymns that helps us to praise and worship

God. And reading the psalms aloud is a good way to say thank you to God.

DID YOU KNOW?

2 CHRONICLES 32:24–26

Hezekiah was a king of Judah, and he was a good king at that. There came a time when Hezekiah became very ill to the point of death . . . and God performed a miracle! But, did you know that Hezekiah didn't thank God? He was too proud to say "thank you"!

Whenever you have a choice between taking credit for something or giving that credit to God, remember: God rewards those who are humble and He punishes those who are proud. Always give God the credit, and let Him give you His blessing.

Spending Time Together

"You know," said Whit, "when I hear you laugh, you remind me of Connie."

Eugene stopped laughing. "I remind you of Connie?" he asked.

Job 33:26

"That's right," Whit answered. "When people spend a lot of time together, they sometimes begin to do the same things."

"I'm well aware of that," Eugene told him. "But I fail to see any similarities between Connie and myself."

Whit winked. "You might be more alike than you think," he said.

It is important that we spend time with God. This will help us to be more like Him. We spend time with God when we read the Bible, when we pray, and when we do His work. God wants us to be like Him—patient, kind, and honest.

A Little Prayer

Dear Lord,

I don't spend nearly as much time with you as I do with my family and friends. I want to change that. I know that you are with me always. So help me to remember to talk with you all day long.

Amen

Memorize Me

He shall pray to God, and He will delight in him, He shall see His face with joy, for He restores to man His righteousness.

JOB 33:26

WORD FOR THE DAY

SIMILARITIES

Similarities is another one of those big, Eugene words. It means "the ways things are alike." Eugene doesn't like to admit it, but he and I are a bit alike. We both help at Whit's End, we both love God, and . . . well . . . I guess we do laugh at the same things, too.

When you look at your family members, you might notice similarities. Maybe you have your mom's nose or your dad's eyes. You might even have a sister or a brother who looks a whole lot like you. Those are all similarities.

The important thing, though, is that there are similarities between God and us. The more time we spend with God, the more we become like Him.

You can spend time with God by reading your Bible. Praying is another great way to be with him. And, since God is everywhere you go, you can spend time with Him any time you like!

DEVOTION

Holly's Special Valentines

Holly sat at a table in Whit's End with colored papers, paste, and crayons surrounding her.

"What are you making?" asked Connie.

James 2:26

"Valentines," answered Holly.

"But Valentine's Day is a long way away," Connie reminded her.

Holly giggled. "I know, but I want to show my friends that I love them. So I'm making 'Anytime Valentines.' They'll be real surprised when they get these."

"Hey, that's a GREAT idea!" Connie said. "Can I help?"

God wants us to show others how much we care for them. And we need to show God that we love Him, too.

A Little Prayer

Dear God,
Thank you for all the people who love me! I love you so much. I don't tell you that as often as I should. I promise to pray more and to read my Bible, just to show you how much I care.
Amen

WORD FOR THE DAY

WORKS

Works is one of those words that can mean many different things. In James 2:26, "works" means "the things that you do." That verse is about the importance of showing our faith through our works. Good works are being kind, sharing, and helping one another. Our works for God are important ways to show Him how much we love Him!

DiD YOU KNOW?

How would you feel if the people you loved never paid any attention to you? I imagine it would hurt. Did you know that God loves us more than anything else? And it's important to love Him in return. God wants us to love him.

I've contemplated how to love God. I pray and I read my Bible to show God that I care. And, sometimes, I just simply utter the words, "I love you, God!" If you take some time to think about it, I'm sure that you too will invent some special ways to show God your love.

Memorize Me

For as the body without the spirit is dead, so faith without works is dead also.
JAMES 2:26

The Moon Rock

Dylan ran over to Eugene. "Look!" he shouted. "Kyle gave me a moon rock."

1 John 2:4–5

Eugene looked at the stone in Dylan's hand. "Have you determined that it's a moon rock?" he asked.

"Yes. Kyle says it was his father's. His dad is an astronaut."

"His dad owns a grocery store," said Eugene. "I used to work for him."

"Oh," said Dylan. "Well, I guess Kyle does tell stories sometimes."

"Is this the same Kyle who saw a mummy in his room?"

"I didn't believe that one," said Dylan.

"Dylan," Eugene said, "perhaps it's time to talk to Kyle about telling the truth."

Remember—trust is earned through actions. It's important to tell the truth.

A Little Prayer

Dear Lord,
Please forgive me for any lies I've told—even the very little ones. I promise to work harder, so that I won't lie any more and other people will trust me. Thank you for your trust, Lord.
Amen

WORD FOR THE DAY

LIAR

A *liar* is someone who tells lies. And a lie is anything that's not true. The Bible says that God doesn't like lies. In fact, God has never, ever told a lie—not even once. So if you want to please God, you must work at telling the truth. And it's okay to remind others to tell the truth, too!

DID YOU KNOW?

You can't build a friendship on dishonesty. A good friend will never lie to you or about you. A good friend will always be loyal.

At times, people will make up stories that are untrue. They might do it to feel important. Or they might do it to stay out of trouble. Whatever the reason, it's wrong to tell a lie.

If you want people to trust you, then you have to be honest. God wants you to be honest so you can be more like Him. God knows how tough it can be to tell the truth all the time. But He'll help you if you only ask Him!

Little by Little

"What are you doing, Mr. Whittaker?" Holly asked.

Luke 17:6

"I'm building a motor for one of my new inventions," Whit said.

"It looks hard," said Holly.

"It's not, really," Whit told her. "It's kind of like faith."

"Like faith?" Holly asked.

Whit smiled. "It takes patience to build this motor. And it takes patience to build your faith, too. But, little by little, if you work at it every day, your faith will grow strong."

God wants us to believe and trust in Him. But we have to learn more about Him each day so our faith can grow stronger.

A Little Prayer

Dear Jesus,

I believe that you lived, that you died for me, and that you rose from the dead. I have faith in you, but please help my faith to grow even stronger. Thank you.

Amen

WORD FOR THE DAY

MUSTARD SEED

Okay, I know—mustard seed—that's actually two words. But together, they are very important. A *mustard seed* is the tiniest of seeds. And Jesus said

Memorize Me

So the Lord said, "If you have faith as a mustard seed, you can say to this mulberry tree, 'Be pulled up by the roots and be planted in the sea,' and it would obey you."

LUKE 17:6

that if your faith is even as small as a mustard seed, it can bring about great things. Do you think you can have this much faith?

DiD YoU KNOW?

Did you know that you have to build your faith? This is how it works:

You believe that Jesus was a real person who lived on earth, who died for you, and who rose from the dead. But that's only the beginning. The more you get to know Jesus, the stronger your faith becomes. That's the building part of it. It means trusting Jesus always. The more you learn about Him, and the more you learn to trust Him, the greater your faith will become.

As Mr. Whittaker says, it happens "little by little" and one day at a time.

How Will You Live Your Life?

Dylan watched as Whit and Eugene played chess. "Will you teach me to play?" he asked.

"Of course," Whit answered. "I'll be happy to teach you the names of the pieces and the directions they move. But I can't tell you each move to make."

Mark 11:22–24

"Why not?" Dylan asked.

"Because chess is a game where *you* make the decisions," Whit said. "You're the only one who can decide where the chess-men will move. It's sort of like living your faith. You are the only one who can decide how to live."

You know how God wants you to behave, but it's up to you to live that way.

A Little Prayer

Dear God,
Thank you for all the possibilities that faith gives me!! I want my faith to grow within me like a seed. I want to live my life in a way that is pleasing to you. Please help me learn to live my faith every day.
Amen

WORD FOR THE DAY

EVIDENCE

Evidence means "proof," something that clearly shows the truth. For example, if there are muddy footprints on the kitchen floor, that is *evidence* that someone didn't take his or her shoes off before walking through. Even though we can't see that person's shoes, we have the proof. In the same way, our faith is *evidence* of our love and belief in God. Our proof that He is always here.

WHIT'S  CORNER

Living Your Faith

JAMES 2

Let's pretend that I invited you over for pizza. But when you got to my house, I wasn't there. Would you still trust me to keep other promises? Now you know I wouldn't do that on purpose, but sometimes unexpected things happen.

Because you trust me, you might have to have faith that I was doing my best to keep my promise. God is like that—we can believe in Him and trust Him. He wants us to have faith.

So whether we're reading the Bible, going to church, following God's commandments, or just being kind to others, we are living our faith. We can live our faith even when we're going to a friend's house for pizza!

FUN TO DO:

Use colored pencils or crayons to write the word "faith." Make each letter a different color. Now use each letter to make a sentence about faith. Start with the letter 'F' and write something like: Focus on God. Now make a sentence using the next letter 'A': Always say your prayers and so on. How else can you show faith?

How Big Is God?

Whit and Jesse were playing checkers.

Psalm 92:8

"Mr. Whittaker? How big is God?" Jesse asked.

"No one knows," Whit said. "He's bigger than we can ever imagine."

"How old is He?" she asked.

"God has been here forever," Whit answered. "So he doesn't have a birthday."

"No birthday!" Jesse cried.

"It's hard to understand, isn't it, Jesse?" Whit said. "But God has always been here, and He will always be here. God is everywhere, and His love lasts forever."

For as long as you live, God will be with you here on earth. And someday you will live with Him forever in heaven.

A Little Prayer

Dear God,

I've learned so many wonderful things about you. The best thing is that you love me. Not only today, but forever. Thank you, God, for loving me and for taking care of me all of the days of my life.

Amen

WORD FOR THE DAY

FOREVERMORE

Forevermore is a wonderful word. It means "always and forever." The Bible says that God will exist forevermore. That means that there will never be a day that God isn't here. He is here to help you, to listen to you, and to love you! His love is yours! For how long? Forevermore!

> ## Memorize Me
> But You, LORD, are on high forevermore.
> PSALM 92:8

DID YOU KNOW?

God's love never had a beginning and it will never end. It has always been here and it will always be! I still haven't totally figured out how that works. But Mr. Whittaker tells me that forever is... well... forever!

So, when do we get to the end of God's love? Never!

That kind of love deserves appreciation. But there's more: The God who loves us forever is also forever good. So when do we get to the end of God's goodness? Never!

Can you imagine being loved forever by a good and loving God? Well, that's what you and I have to look forward to. When we believe in Jesus and trust in Him, then we will be with God forever.

Index

More about Odyssey

John Avery Whittaker

I used to be a junior high school teacher, but I've been a sailor, a soldier, an encyclopedia publisher, and a computer programmer. I was even a camp director at Camp What-A-Nut. Now I run Whit's End, a discovery emporium for kids and a soda shop where Connie and Eugene work. I love to see my friends who visit me at Whit's End. They come for the company, the inventions, and the ice cream!

Connie Kendall

I LOVE kids, and someday I want to be a teacher . . . or maybe a playwright or even a director. I really do love the movies. But I don't like house-work. And I'm not a very good cook. My favorite place in the whole world is the beach, although we don't have one here in Odyssey. Oh yeah, Eugene is my good friend, but he really gets on my nerves when he uses great, big words all the time.

Eugene Meltsner

I enjoy literature, computers, law, history, and all the sciences. I started high school when I was nine and graduated at age twelve. I've been studying computer programming in college for many years, and I'm already an inventor. I ride a bike everywhere I go because it is safe and economical. Oh yeah, Miss Kendall is my good friend, but she really grates my nerves when she uses incorrect grammar.

Dylan Taylor

I'm ten years old, and I love new stuff. My mom says that I'm adventurous, but really I'm good at knowing how to have fun, especially when I find something mysterious. And I like to do stuff with Carter and Sal—they're my best friends. My little sister Jesse bugs me sometimes, but I love her. I hang around Whit's End a lot because there's always something interesting going on.

Jesse Taylor

I'm seven. I love to play with my toys best of all. I like to play in my brother Dylan's room, too, but he doesn't let me. He makes me leave and tells me to go play with my dolls. But sometimes I don't get out, so Dylan tells Mom or Dad. Dylan says my dolls are disgusting. I really love to play with our dog, Sherman. He was a present to me and Dylan from Mr. Whittaker.

Sherman
Woof. Woof. Woof.

Jasper
Meow. Meow. Meow.

Holly Ferguson

I live next door to Dylan and Jesse. People call me a tomboy, but I don't care. I can do anything as good as anybody else. My favorite place is my tree house. I love going up there, and I even built most of it all by myself. And I love my cat. Her name is Jasper, and at first, she didn't like Dylan or Sherman. I really like going to Whit's End, too. Mostly because I really love to see Connie.

Carter Williams

I'm ten. I love being the center of attention, but only if everybody's laughing real hard. Mr. Whittaker thinks that I'll probably grow up to be a comedian. I am thinking about a career in entertainment. Or maybe I'll do professional negotiating, because I'm really good at it. Like, whenever Sal and Dylan get into a big argument, I'm always the one who smoothes things out. Really, I am.

Sal Martinez

I'm nine years old, and I love to read. I can remember facts and figures after I've only seen or heard them one time. And I'm really good with computers, too. I'm in the same class as Dylan and Carter because I got to skip a grade. Sometimes Dylan gets mad at me because I am a cautious person. I like to think about things for awhile before I make a decision. Mr. Whittaker says I like to look before I leap.